i

The Cashflow Blueprint for Coaches and Consultants

How to Standout and Crush Sales in a Crowded Market

By Dr. Jamar Suber

The Cashflow Blueprint for Coaches & Consultants:
How To Standout and Crush Sales in A Crowded Market
Published by ICXII Publishing
1348 Beach Blvd, Jacksonville Beach FL 32240 USA
Copyright © 2023 Dr. Jamar Suber. All Rights Reserved

ISBN: 979-8-9916585-0-8

Contact Information:
Dr. Jamar Suber
Email: cambryia.dinee@jamarsuber.com

Have Questions? Book A Call with Dr. Suber For Your VIP Business Audit Today!
VIP Business Audit Call

Dedication

To the billions of struggling Coaches and
Consultants that have purchased this book.

May The Force Be With You **- Star Wars**

Table of Contents

"Your story isn't just your past; it's your power to connect and convert."

Chapter 1:
Embrace Growth from Every Failure

So, here we are at the beginning of this journey together. Before we get into the strategies, systems, and tactics that will elevate your coaching business to a level where cash flow is constant and sales are soaring, we've got to get real. We have to take a hard look in the mirror, face the music, and assess where you fell short. This isn't about beating yourself up. No, it's about owning your story and using it to catapult yourself to new heights. Because if there's one thing I know for sure, it's that our steps are ordered by God. Even when we face adversity, even when we stumble, God is still guiding us. Your setbacks? They're just setups for your comeback. And today, we're going to embrace that truth and move forward with a relentless spirit.

Assess Where You've Fallen Short

I remember when I first realized I had been falling short in my journey. It wasn't pretty. I had built up this coaching business, thinking I was doing everything right. I had a brand, a following, and even a few wins under my belt. But the reality was that my cash flow was inconsistent, my sales were shaky, and there were more days of self-doubt than I care to admit. I was living on potential, but not walking on purpose. And that's a dangerous place to be.

See, I've been knocked down more times than I can count. I've been flat on my back with no idea how I was going to get back up. There was a time when I lost everything. My business was crumbling, my marriage was falling apart, and my spirit was broken. I felt like I was running on empty, trying to keep up appearances while drowning inside. I'd built a nice façade, but behind the scenes, the foundation was cracking.

Get Up and Dust Yourself Off

Now, if you've ever been in that place where life hits you so hard that you don't even know where to start again, you'll know what I'm talking about. It's in those moments, when you're on the ground, that you have a decision to make. You can either stay down and let life steamroll over you, or you can get up, dust yourself off, and decide that this is not how your story ends.

I remember that night after my car accident when I could have given up. I had made some bad choices, and gotten caught up in things that were pulling me further from my purpose. I remember the silence after the crash—the kind of silence that's almost deafening. My mind was spinning, trying to make sense of what happened, and all I could think was, "God, how did I end up here?" But even in that moment, I felt something stirring in my spirit. It was a small voice saying,

"Get up. This isn't the end."

I believe that God orders our steps, even when we think we're lost. Even when we mess up, when we fall short, when we can't see the way forward—He's still there, ordering each step. That night, lying in that hospital bed, I made a choice. I chose to get up, to dust myself off, and to keep going. And let me tell you, that decision changed everything.

Quiet the Noise, Go Against the Grain, and Become Relentless

But here's the thing: getting up is just the first step. When you've been knocked down, you've got to quiet the noise around you—the voices that tell you you're not good enough, that you can't make it, that you're too far gone. You've got to shut that noise down and decide to go against the grain. Decide to become relentless.

When I started building my coaching brand from scratch, I realized I had to do things differently. I couldn't follow the same tired formula everyone else was using. I had to go against the grain. I had to quiet the noise of what everyone else thought I should be doing and tune into what God was telling me to do.

I'm not going to sugarcoat it—it wasn't easy. I faced criticism. I faced doubt. People said I was crazy for leaving behind what was "safe" and diving headfirst into the unknown. But I knew that to get what I'd never had, I had to do what I'd never done. I had to be relentless in pursuing the vision God had placed in my heart.

It's like when I started my first business selling pagers. I was just a kid, 16 years old, but I saw an opportunity. I went against the grain. I didn't have the knowledge or the experience, but I had the drive. I had the grit. And when people told me it wasn't going to work, I blocked out the noise and went after it anyway. That business taught me a lot about what it means to be relentless—about the kind of tenacity it takes to succeed.

And guess what? The same principles apply to your coaching business today.

To stand out in a crowded market, you have to stop trying to be like everyone else. You have to find your voice, and your unique story, and be relentless in sharing it with the world. You've got to get up every day with a hunger to serve, to impact, and to create something bigger than yourself.

Adversity as a Divine Setup

Now, let's talk about adversity. I believe with everything in me that God allows adversity to shape us, to mold us, and to prepare us for what's next. When I think about all the times I've faced adversity—whether it was losing a business, facing personal betrayal, or staring down the aftermath of bad decisions—I realize now that it was all a divine setup.

I remember running a magazine back in Pittsburgh. Man, that thing blew up. We were on the radio, on TV, doing interviews, signing autographs—I thought I was on top of the world. But then, just like that, it all came crashing down. Bad partnerships, financial missteps, and a market that moved faster than we did. I could've stayed stuck in disappointment, but I chose to see it differently. I chose to see it as God redirecting my steps, pushing me out of what was comfortable and into what was necessary for my growth.

You see, the key is not to avoid adversity but to learn how to leverage it. Adversity will either break you or build you, and the choice is yours. I realized that every setback was setting me up for something greater. Every failure was a lesson in disguise. And if you're willing to look at your challenges with that mindset, you'll start to see that nothing is wasted in God's plan.

Get Back Up—Every Time

The only way you fail is if you refuse to get back up. In this life, and especially in this business, you will get knocked down. You will face disappointments, rejection, and moments where you feel like quitting. But let me tell you something—there's power in getting back up.

I'm reminded of the story of my Aunt Carol. She was like a second mother to me, and when she passed, it felt like the wind had been knocked out of me. I could've stayed in that place of grief, but I knew she wouldn't want that. I knew I had to get back up, keep going, and keep building. I took that pain and turned it into purpose. I used it to fuel my next move, to propel me forward when everything in me wanted to give up.

The same goes for you. Whatever you're facing—whether it's financial struggles, a lack of clarity, or the weight of life's hardships—you've got to decide to get back up. Dust yourself off. Refocus. And get back in the game.

Because here's the thing: your purpose is too big, your calling is too great, and your impact is too important to stay down. You've got lives to change, clients to serve, and a legacy to build. So, no matter how many times you get knocked down, commit to getting back up every single time.

Becoming Relentless

To stand out in a crowded market, you have to be relentless. And I'm not talking about hustle culture or grinding yourself into the ground. I'm talking about a relentless commitment to your calling, to your clients, and to the work God has called you to do.

I've always believed that the secret to success is staying in the game longer than anyone else is willing to. It's about showing up, day after day, when you're tired when you're frustrated, and when nothing seems to be working. It's about having the kind of grit that refuses to back down, no matter how tough the road gets.

When I ruptured my Achilles tendon, not once but twice, it would have been easy to sit on the sidelines. I was in pain—physical, emotional, and spiritual pain. But I had to dig deep. I had to find that place within me that said, "You are not done yet." And that's where I want you to get to today. A place where you become relentless in the pursuit of what God has called you to do.

So, how do you become relentless? You keep going. You keep pushing. You keep learning, adapting, and growing. You don't let setbacks deter you; you let them define you. You let them make you stronger, wiser, and more determined than ever.

Embracing the Assessment

So, let's get back to where we started—assessing where you fell short. If you're serious about creating cash flow mastery in your coaching business, you've got to be honest about what's not working. This isn't the time to be soft or sugarcoat things. This is where you pull back the curtain and get real about what's holding you back.

Maybe you've been inconsistent with your messaging. One day you're talking about empowerment; the next, you're talking about productivity hacks. Your audience is confused because you're confused. Or maybe you've been avoiding sales because you hate the idea of being "salesy." Trust me, I've been there. I used to think if I just put out good content, the clients would come. But the truth is if you don't know how to sell, you're leaving money—and impact—on the table.

You've got to assess where you've been hiding, where you've been playing small, and where you've been afraid to step into the fullness of who you are as a coach. And let's be clear: there is no shame in falling short. The only shame is in refusing to learn from it.

Final Thoughts: Embrace the Process

As we close this chapter, I want you to take a moment and reflect on where you've fallen short. Not from a place of shame, but from a place of growth. Assess where you are, get up, dust yourself off, and quiet the noise. Go against the grain and decide right here, right now, to become relentless.

Remember, your steps are ordered by God. Every failure, every setback, every challenge—it's all part of the plan. And if you're willing to stay in the game, to keep pushing forward, and to trust that God is guiding you, there is nothing you can't overcome.

This is just the beginning, and there's so much more ahead. Let's build, let's grow, and let's crush it—together. Your Cash Flow Blueprint starts now.

Here is an assessment designed to help business coaches reflect on their experiences with failure, including common frustrations, desires, and fears. The table is structured to allow the reader to identify and explore their feelings and thoughts. Each table provides space for introspection and planning for overcoming challenges.

*"The most powerful marketing tool
is a client who can't stop talking
about their transformation."*

Instructions for Use:

Frustrations: Reflect on and list the top frustrations you've faced in your coaching business related to failures or setbacks.

_____
_____
_____
_____
_____
_____

How Do I Overcome? Use this section to brainstorm potential strategies, actions, or mindset shifts needed to overcome these challenges and fears.

_____
_____
_____
_____
_____
_____

Fears: Identify the fears that come up when you think about your frustrations and desires. What's holding you back or causing hesitation?

_____
_____
_____
_____
_____
_____

Desire: Consider what you truly desire to achieve in your coaching what goals or outcomes would resolve these frustrations?

_____

_____

_____

_____

_____

_____

By filling out these tables, coaches can gain greater self-awareness, identify actionable steps for growth, and develop a more focused strategy for achieving success in their business.

Assessment Table for Coaches in Business

X- Axis	Frustrations	Desires	Fears	How Do I Overcome?
No. 1	Inconsistent cash flow and unpredictable income streams	To have a stable and predictable income	Fear of financial instability and failure	
No.2	Difficulty in attracting and retaining ideal clients	To build a loyal and engaged client base	Fear of not being able to find enough clients to sustain the business	
No. 3	Lack of clarity on brand positioning and unique value proposition	To have a clear, strong, and differentiated brand	Fear of blending in and not standing out in a crowded market	
No. 4	Overwhelmed from wearing too many hats (marketing, sales, coaching)	To delegate and build a reliable team	Fear of losing control or quality when delegating tasks	
No. 5	Ineffective marketing strategies leading to poor visibility	To have a strong online presence and attract organic traffic	Fear of wasting time and money on ineffective marketing efforts	
No. 6	Struggles with closing sales and converting leads	To master sales techniques that feel authentic and effective	Fear of coming across as "salesy" or pushy	
No. 7	Difficulty setting and maintaining healthy boundaries	To have a balanced workload and personal life	Fear of burnout or losing passion for coaching	
No. 8	Inconsistent client results lead to a lack of testimonials and referrals	To achieve consistent client success and satisfaction	Fear of being perceived as ineffective or inexperienced	
No. 9	Navigating negative feedback or criticism from clients	To be recognized as a credible authority in their field	Fear of negative reviews damaging reputation	
No. 10	Difficulty staying motivated during periods of low sales	To maintain a resilient mindset and drive through challenges	Fear of long-term business failure due to lack of growth	

19

Blank Assessment Table for Independent Reflection

X axis	Frustrations	Desires	Fears	How Do I Over Come?
No. 1				
No. 2				
No. 3				
No. 4				
No. 5				
No. 6				
No. 7				
No. 8				
No. 9				
No. 10				

"Failures are the stepping-stones that lead to a relentless pursuit of greatness."

Chapter 2:
Relentless Begins Within

So, we're diving deep now. You've made it this far, and that tells me you're serious about taking your coaching business—and your life—to the next level. In this chapter, we're talking about how to become relentless. But before we get into strategies and steps, let's get one thing clear: being relentless isn't about grinding yourself into the ground. It's about knowing who you are, who you are, and what you've been called to do. It's about a fire that doesn't burn out, a commitment that doesn't waver, and a faith that doesn't fold. It's about becoming unstoppable in the pursuit of your God-given purpose.

Being Relentless Starts with Believing in Who God Created You to Be

It all begins with belief. Not just any belief, but belief in who God created you to be. See, many of us are out here chasing dreams, goals, and visions, but we're trying to do it on shaky ground. We haven't yet come to fully believe in the masterpiece God made when He made us. The Bible says in Psalm 139:14, "I praise you because I am fearfully and wonderfully made; your works are wonderful, I know that full well." God didn't create you haphazardly. He took His time with you.

You are fearfully and wonderfully made, crafted with intentionality and purpose.

For the longest time, I struggled with this. I grew up feeling like I had to prove myself. I wanted to be liked, to be seen, to be acknowledged. I found myself constantly hustling for my worthiness—trying to impress people, trying to live up to their expectations. But here's the problem: when you try to define yourself by what others think, you end up becoming a shadow of who God called you to be. And a shadow has no substance.

I remember a time in my life when I was trying to make everyone around me happy. I had this magazine in Pittsburgh, and we were on fire. Radio, TV, signing autographs—it felt like I was on top of the world. But deep down, I knew something was off. I was so busy chasing the applause of men that I lost sight of what God was calling me to do. And let me tell you, that's a dangerous place to be. It wasn't until everything came crashing down that I realized I'd been building my house on sand. When you build on sand, it only takes one storm to knock it all down.

God had to remind me of who I was and who I was. He had to remind me that my identity wasn't in what I accomplished, but in who He created me to be. That's when I began to understand what it means to be relentless. It starts with a deep, unshakeable belief in the Creator and the creation—YOU. When you know that you are made in His image, you stop allowing the world to define you. You stop letting people's opinions dictate your actions. You stop chasing validation from man because you're already validated by God.

Being relentless means standing firm in that belief. It means waking up every day knowing that you were created for a purpose, that God doesn't make mistakes, and that He doesn't create anything without value. When you walk in that truth, you become unstoppable. You start to see that everything you need to succeed is already inside you because God put it there.

God Created You and Broke the Mold

Here's the thing: when God created you, He broke the mold. He never created another you. You are a one-of-one, a unique masterpiece, crafted by the hands of The Almighty. Ephesians 2:10 says, "For we are God's handiwork, created in Christ Jesus to do good works, which God prepared in advance for us to do." You were designed with a purpose that no one else on this earth can fulfill. There's no other person who can bring what you bring to the table. And that's why following God's leading is so crucial.

Too many of us fall into the trap of trying to follow man's path instead of God's. We look around, see what's working for others, and we think, "Well, maybe I should do that too." But God is saying, "I didn't call you to be them; I called you to be you." When we start trying to live up to the expectations of others, we miss the mark. We end up frustrated, drained, and unfulfilled because we're out of alignment with God's plan.

I know this all too well. There was a season in my life when I was more focused on what people thought of me than on what God said about me. I was trying to be everything to everyone—trying to fit into boxes that people created for me. But God doesn't operate in boxes. He operates in purpose. And purpose doesn't always fit neatly into the world's expectations.

When I finally got tired of pleasing man, I had to make a decision. I had to decide to follow God's leading, even when it didn't make sense to anyone else. Even when people said I was crazy, I had to trust that God's way is where peace is found. Because let me tell you, the peace that comes from being in alignment with God's will is unmatched. It's the kind of peace that surpasses all understanding

(Philippians 4:7).

Following God's leading took me to places I never would have gone on my own.

It took me from Pittsburgh to Jacksonville, where I knew no one and had nothing. But I knew God was calling me there. It didn't make sense to the people around me. They thought I was losing it. But I had to trust that God was ordering my steps. And you know what? He was. When I look back now, I see how He was positioning me, preparing me, and setting me up for a season of growth that I never could have imagined.

So, here's my challenge to you: stop trying to fit in. Stop trying to please everyone around you. Stop chasing the applause of man and start seeking the approval of God. Follow His leading and watch how your life begins to transform. The people you lose along the way. They were never meant to go where God is taking you. The opportunities that pass you by? God has something better. When you're aligned with His will, you find peace, clarity, and a relentless drive that propels you forward.

Understand That Failure is Fuel to Propel You Higher

If you want to become relentless, you've got to change the way you see failure. Too many of us see failure as the end when it's just the beginning. Failure isn't final; it's fuel. It's the thing God uses to propel us higher, to shape us, and to sharpen us for His use.

I've failed more times than I can count. I've failed in business, I've failed in relationships, and I've even failed myself. But I've come to understand that every failure was necessary. Every failure was part of the process. Romans 8:28 reminds us, "And we know that in all things God works for the good of those who love him, who have been called according to his purpose." God doesn't waste anything—not even your failures. He uses them to refine you, to mold you, and to prepare you for what's next.

Think about the story of Joseph in the Bible. He was betrayed by his own brothers, thrown into a pit, sold into slavery, falsely accused, and thrown into prison. At any point, Joseph could have given up. He could have said, "God, I'm done. This isn't fair." But he didn't. He remained faithful, and in the end, God elevated him to a position of power and influence. What the enemy meant for evil, God used for good (Genesis 50:20).

When I look back over my own life, I see how God has done the same for me. There were times when I thought I was done times when I thought I had failed beyond repair. But God had other plans. He used every failure to strengthen me, to teach me, and to build me up. He used every setback as a setup for something greater.

One of those times was when I ruptured my Achilles tendon—twice. I had been building my business, things were moving, and then suddenly, I found myself laid up, unable to move, feeling like my world had come crashing down. I felt like I had lost everything. But it was in that stillness, in that place of pain, that God started to speak to me. He reminded me that He was still in control, that He was still ordering my steps, and that this was just another chapter in my story.

It was then that I realized failure wasn't the end; it was the fuel. It was what God was using to propel me higher. He was sharpening me, refining me, and preparing me for the next level. And that's the mindset you have to adopt if you want to be relentless. You have to see failure as part of the process. You have to understand that God orders failure to shape you and sharpen you for His use. You have to keep going, keep pushing, and keep believing that there's something greater on the other side.

Being Relentless Means Do Not Stop

Being relentless means, you don't stop. You don't quit. You don't give up when things get hard. You don't throw in the towel when the road gets rough. You keep moving forward, step by step, day by day, trusting that God is guiding you every step of the way.

I'm reminded of Galatians 6:9, which says, "Let us not become weary in doing good, for at the proper time we will reap a harvest if we do not give up." That's a promise right there. If you don't give up, you will reap a harvest. It may not come when you want it, and it may not look the way you expected, but it will come.

I've seen this play out in my life over and over again. When I was building my security business from the ground up, there were so many times I wanted to quit. I was working for $9.15 an hour, people thought I was crazy, and nothing seemed to be happening. But I kept going. I kept believing. I kept trusting that God had a plan.

And He did. Eventually, that little $ 9.15-an-hour job turned into a seven-figure business. Not because I was so smart, not because I had it all figured out, but because I refused to quit.

And that's what I want for you. I want you to become relentless in the pursuit of your God-given purpose. I want you to keep going when the road gets tough, to keep pushing when you feel like you've got nothing left, to keep believing even when everything around you says it's impossible.

Because here's the truth: God didn't bring you this far to leave you. He didn't create you, break the mold, and call you by name just to watch you fail. He's got a plan for you—a plan to prosper you and not to harm you, a plan to give you hope and a future (Jeremiah 29:11).

So, don't stop. Don't quit. Don't give up. Be relentless. Keep moving forward, and watch how God takes you from glory to glory, strength to strength, and victory to victory.

Final Thoughts: The Relentless Mindset

As we wrap up this chapter, I want you to take a moment and reflect on what it means to be relentless. It's not just a word; it's a way of life. It's a mindset that says, "I will not be moved. I will not be shaken. I will not be stopped." It's a commitment to God, to yourself, and to the people you've been called to serve.

Remember, being relentless starts with believing in who God created you to be. It means knowing that He broke the mold when He made you, that you are fearfully and wonderfully made, and that you have a unique purpose that no one else can fulfill. It means following God's leading, even when it doesn't make sense, and understanding that His way is where peace is found. And it means seeing failure not as the end, but as fuel—fuel to propel you higher, to sharpen you, and to prepare you for what's next.

So, let's go. Let's be relentless. Let's refuse to quit. Let's follow God's lead and walk boldly in the purpose He's laid out for us. Your best days are ahead, and with God by your side, there's nothing you can't overcome.

Your journey to becoming relentless starts now. Here is an assessment designed to help coaches reflect on their experiences and challenges when trying to shift from people-pleasing to focusing on pleasing God. The table includes common frustrations, desires, and fears that coaches may encounter during this transition. Each table provides space for introspection and planning to overcome these challenges.

"A relentless mindset begins when you stop seeking approval and start seeking purpose."

Instructions for Use:

Frustrations: Reflect on and list the frustrations you have faced or are currently facing in your coaching journey related to transitioning from people-pleasing to pleasing God.

Desires: Identify your core desires and goals that are rooted in aligning with God's will and not the expectations of others.

Fears: Pinpoint the fears that emerge when thinking about moving away from seeking approval from people and turning towards seeking God's approval.

How Do I Overcome? Use this section to develop actionable strategies, prayer points, or mindset shifts needed to overcome these challenges and live more authentically in your calling.

By filling out these tables, coaches can gain deeper insights into their inner conflicts, realign their focus towards pleasing God, and create a more purposeful approach to their personal and professional lives.

Example Assessment Table for Coaches Shifting from People-Pleasing to Pleasing God

X- Axis	Frustrations	Desires	Fears	How Do I Overcome?
No. 1	Feeling overwhelmed by others' expectations and demands	To experience freedom from the need for approval	Fear of losing clients or relationships by setting boundaries	
No. 2	Constantly second-guessing decisions to avoid disappointing others	To gain confidence in making decisions aligned with God's will	Fear of judgment or criticism from peers or clients	
No. 3	Lack of clarity in personal and professional identity	To discover and embrace a true, God-centered identity	Fear of not being understood or accepted in their authenticity	
No. 4	Struggling to say "no" and overcommitting to please others	To have the courage to prioritize God's calling above all else	Fear of missing out on opportunities or Potential growth	
No. 5	Feeling drained by trying to meet everyone's expectations	To find peace and fulfillment in pleasing God alone	Fear of being seen as selfish or uncooperative	
No. 6	Difficulty in setting and maintaining healthy boundaries	To build meaningful and God-centered relationships	Fear of isolation or being left out of social or professional circles	
No. 7	Emotional exhaustion from trying to be "Everything to everyone"	To feel spiritually grounded and emotionally balanced	Fear of failure if they don't meet others' expectations	
No. 8	Confusion over conflicting advice or opinions from others	To have clarity and trust in God's guidance above all	Fear of not having a clear path if they don't rely on others' opinions	
No. 9	Perceiving success as dependent on others' approval	To redefine success according to God's standards	Fear of not achieving worldly success or recognition	
No. 10	Inability to let go of the need for validation from others	To fully rely on God for approval and worth	Fear of not being "good enough" in God's eyes or their own	

Blank Assessment Table for Independent Reflection

X-Axis	Frustrations	Desires	Fears	How Do I Overcome?
No. 1				
No. 2				
No. 3				
No. 4				
No. 5				
No. 6				
No. 7				
No. 8				
No. 9				
No. 10				

31

"Know your audience, and you'll
never run out of clients who
need your gift."

Chapter 3: Know Your Audience

If you're serious about building a coaching business that thrives—one that stands out in a crowded market, attracts the right clients, and generates consistent cash flow—then you've got to know your audience. I'm not talking about having a vague idea of who might be interested in your services. I'm talking about deeply understanding who you are called to serve, what their pain points are, where they hang out, and how you can speak directly to their needs in a way that grabs their attention and moves them to action.

In this chapter, we're diving deep into the art and science of knowing your audience. Because if you don't know who you're targeting, you'll end up targeting no one. If you're shooting in the dark, don't be surprised when you miss the mark. So, let's get clear. Let's define it. Let's break it down. Let's get strategic about how to attract the clients who need you most and who are ready to invest in what you have to offer.

Target Marketing: Definition, Explanation, and Importance of

First things first: What is target marketing? Target marketing is the process of identifying a specific group of people who are most likely to benefit from your services and crafting your messaging, content, and offers specifically for them. It's about narrowing down your focus so that you can hit the bullseye rather than scattering your energy and resources all over the place.

Imagine you're out fishing. You wouldn't throw your net into an empty pond and expect to catch something, would you? No, you'd go where the fish are, use the right bait, and cast your net with intention. The same principle applies to marketing your coaching business. You need to know where your "fish" are—your ideal clients. You need to understand what they're hungry for, what keeps them up at night, what their hopes and dreams are, and what they're willing to invest in to solve their problems.

Many coaches make the mistake of trying to appeal to everyone. They're afraid to niche down because they think it will limit their opportunities. But here's the truth: When you try to speak to everyone, you end up speaking to no one. Your message gets diluted, and it doesn't resonate with anyone.

Target marketing isn't about exclusion; it's about precision. It's about crafting a message that is so clear, so specific, and so compelling that the right people can't help but take notice.

Let me break it down a bit more. Target marketing involves three key components:

Identifying Your Ideal Client (Avatar): Who are you called to serve? What are their demographics (age, gender, location, income level)? What are their psychographics (beliefs, values, interests, challenges)? What are their biggest pain points, and what solutions are they actively seeking?

Creating a Customer Journey: Where does your ideal client hang out? What platforms do they use? What content are they consuming? How can you strategically position yourself in those spaces to become a trusted authority in their eyes?

Crafting Targeted Messaging: How do you speak their language? How do you connect with them on an emotional level? What stories can you share that will resonate with their experiences and aspirations? The goal is to make them feel like, "This coach gets me; they understand my struggles, and they have the solution I've been looking for."

Understanding and implementing these three components is crucial because it allows you to focus your energy and resources where they will have the greatest impact. It's the difference between throwing spaghetti at the wall to see what sticks and executing a strategic, results-driven marketing plan that attracts your ideal clients like a magnet.

The Bullseye Analogy—Hitting the Target

Now, let me paint a picture for you to drive this home. Imagine you're standing at a gun range. In front of you is a target with multiple rings and a bright red center dot— the bullseye. Your goal is to hit that red center dot. You want to aim carefully, steady your hands, and pull the trigger with precision to hit that bullseye. But while you're shooting, you'll notice that some of your shots will hit other spots on the target. Some may hit the outer rings; others might be closer to the center but still not quite there. That's okay because the goal is to keep adjusting your aim until you start consistently hitting that bullseye.

Now, let's apply this analogy to your coaching business and your marketing strategy. The red center dot represents your ideal client, those who are the perfect fit for your services, who are ready and willing to invest, who see the value you bring, and who align with your mission and values. These are the clients you're aiming to attract.

However, while you're aiming for that ideal client, you will inevitably attract others who aren't perfect fit but who still resonate with some aspects of your message. They're like the outer rings of the target. They're still on board; they're still in your orbit. Sometimes, these clients may still be worth serving, or they may lead to referrals or other opportunities.

The key is to keep your focus on that bullseye. Keep refining your messaging, your offers, and your strategy until you start consistently attracting those ideal clients. When you start hitting that red center dot regularly, that's when you know you've nailed your target marketing. That's when your cash flow starts to stabilize, your sales start to soar, and your impact starts to multiply.

But here's the reality: You're going to miss sometimes. Not every ad campaign will hit the mark. Not every piece of content will resonate. Not every client will be a perfect fit. And that's okay. It's part of the process. The goal is to keep shooting, to keep refining, and to keep learning from each shot, each campaign, and each client interaction. You take the data, you analyze it, and you adjust your aim. You don't stop shooting; you get better with every shot.

I remember when I first started in business. I had this vision of the ideal clients I wanted to serve. But I didn't know exactly how to reach them, what message would resonate, or what platforms they were on. So, I tried a little bit of everything. I shot at different targets, tested different messages, and explored different platforms. Some hit, and many missed. But with each shot, I got clearer. I started to understand who my audience was, where they were, and how to speak directly to their needs. And when I did, everything changed.

You've got to be willing to go through that process, to stay in the game, and to keep aiming for that bullseye. Because when you hit it. the reward is worth every shot.

I Am Giving You $10K to Spend on Ads.

Alright, let's get practical. I'm giving you $10,000 to spend on ads. Where would you spend that money, and why? Now, before you start throwing money at Facebook or Google Ads let's take a step back and think strategically. Because it's not just about spending money, it's about spending money wisely.

When it comes to running ads, the first thing you need to know is where your audience is hanging out. Are they on Facebook, Instagram, LinkedIn,

YouTube, or somewhere else? The platform you choose will depend on the demographics and behaviors of your target audience. If your ideal clients are corporate professionals looking for executive coaching, you might lean towards LinkedIn. If you're targeting a younger demographic interested in lifestyle coaching, Instagram might be your go to. If you're offering comprehensive training or workshops, YouTube or Facebook might be more suitable.

Here's how I would break it down:

Facebook and Instagram Ads (50% of Budget - $5,000):

Facebook and Instagram are powerful platforms for building brand awareness and driving targeted traffic to your coaching business. These platforms allow you to create highly targeted ads based on interests, demographics, behaviors, and even lookalike audiences. You can use this $5,000 to run a series of ads that focus on different stages of the customer journey—awareness, engagement, and conversion.

Create ads that speak directly to the pain points and desires of your ideal clients. Use compelling visuals, strong headlines, and clear calls to action. Facebook and Instagram also allow you to retarget people who have visited your website or engaged with your content, which is crucial for converting prospects into clients.

LinkedIn Ads (20% of Budget - $2,000):

If you're in the B2B coaching space, LinkedIn is a goldmine. It's the platform where professionals hang out, network, and look for business solutions. Use LinkedIn ads to target decision-makers, HR managers, executives, and other professionals who could benefit from your coaching services. The key on LinkedIn is to offer value first. Run ads that promote a free webinar, a downloadable guide, or a case study that showcases your expertise and positions you as an authority in your niche. This not only builds trust but also generates qualified leads who are more likely to convert.

Google Ads (20% of Budget - $2,000):

Google Ads are powerful for capturing intent. When someone is actively searching for a solution to their problem, they're more likely to be ready to invest in a coaching program. Use Google Ads to target high-intent keywords related to your coaching niche. For example, if you're a business coach, you might target keywords like "business coach for entrepreneurs," "executive coaching services," or "how to scale my business." The goal is to appear at the top of search results when your ideal clients are

Here is a comprehensive fill-in-the-blank worksheet designed to help coaches define their target market by identifying key demographic categories. Each category provides a specific area for coaches to consider as they narrow down their ideal client profile.

Final Notes for Coaches:

After completing this worksheet, review your answers and create a comprehensive profile or "avatar" of your ideal client. This will help you better understand their needs, preferences, and where to find them. Knowing these details will allow you to create targeted content, offers, and marketing strategies that resonate deeply with your audience.

"Your brand isn't just a logo--It's the experience and emotion people feel when they encounter you."

Breakout Exercise

Target Market Demographic Worksheet for Coaches

Instructions: Fill in the blanks for each demographic category to clearly define the target market for your coaching business. The more specific you are, the better you will understand who you are serving and how to reach them effectively.

Age Range:
The ideal age range of my target audience is _____ to _____ years old.

Gender:
The primary gender I am targeting is _____ (Male, Female, Non-binary, Other).

Race/Ethnicity:
The primary race/ethnicity of my target audience is _____ (e.g., Caucasian, Black/African American, Hispanic/Latino, Asian, Native American, Mixed, Other).

Sexual Orientation/Preference:
The sexual orientation/preference of my target audience is _____ (e.g., Heterosexual, Homosexual, Bisexual, Asexual, Pansexual, Other).

Marital Status:
The marital status of my ideal client is _____ (e.g., Single, Married, Divorced, Widowed, In a Relationship, Other).

Household Size:
The average household size of my target audience is _____ (e.g., Single, Couple, Family with children, Other).

Parental Status:
My ideal client is likely to have _____ (e.g., No children, young children, Teenagers, Adult children, Empty nester).

Education Level:
The education level of my target audience is _____ (e.g., High school diploma, associate degree, bachelor's degree, master's degree, Doctorate, Other).

Occupation/Industry:
My ideal client typically works in the _____ industry (e.g., Healthcare, Finance, Education, Tech, Retail, Other) and holds positions such as _____.

Income Level:
The typical annual income range of my target audience is _____ (e.g., Under $30,000, $30,000-$50,000, $50,000-$75,000, $75,000-$100,000, Over $100,000).

Geographic Location:
My target audience is primarily located in _____ (e.g., Urban areas, Suburban areas, Rural areas, Specific city/state/country).

Cultural Background:
The cultural background of my target audience is _____ (e.g., Western, Eastern, Middle Eastern, Latino, African, Other).

Language Spoken:
My target audience primarily speaks _____ (e.g., English, Spanish, Mandarin, French, Other).

Religion/Belief System:
The predominant religion or belief system of my target market is _____ (e.g., Christianity, Islam, Hinduism, Buddhism, Judaism, Agnostic, Atheist, Other).

Hobbies/Interests:
Common hobbies and interests of my ideal clients include _____ (e.g., Fitness, Reading, Traveling, Cooking, Music, Other).

Political Views:
My target audience tends to have _____ political views (e.g., Conservative, Liberal, Moderate, Apolitical, Other).

Tech Savviness:
The typical level of tech savviness among my target audience is _____ (e.g., Low, Medium, High).

Preferred Content Consumption Channels:
My audience consumes content primarily on _____ (e.g., Facebook, Instagram, LinkedIn, YouTube, Podcasts, Blogs, Newsletters, Other).

Media Preferences:
My target audience prefers _____ (e.g., Video, Audio, Written articles, Infographics, Webinars, E-books, and others).

Buying Behavior:
My ideal clients prefer to make purchases _____ (e.g., Online, In-person, through referrals, after attending a webinar, Other).

Psychographic Traits:
Key psychographic traits of my target audience include _____ (e.g., Ambitious, Family-oriented, Health-conscious, Risk-averse, Trendsetter, Other).

Pain Points and Challenges:
The primary pain points and challenges faced by my target market are _____ (e.g., Work-life balance, Career growth, financial stability, Health and wellness, Personal development, and others).

"If you're not telling your story, you're leaving your legacy in someone else's hands."

Chapter 4:
Narrative Mastery: How to Make Your Story Connect and Convert

---

Here we go, diving deep into one of the most powerful tools in your arsenal as a coach: your story. If you've been following along, you already know we've talked about getting clear on your target market and understanding the relentless mindset you need to thrive. But now, we need to talk about the heart of your business, the unique story that only you can tell. Your story carries weight. It holds value. And if you learn how to use it correctly, it can turn potential clients into raving fans who can't wait to work with you.

The Value of Your Story

Let's get one thing straight: **your story has value**. I'm not talking about the kind of value that fades over time. I'm talking about the deep, transformational value that carries the keys to unlocking someone else's breakthrough. Your story is your power, and it's uniquely yours. Nobody else on this planet has lived your exact experience, faced your unique challenges, or come out the other side with the lessons you've learned. That's why your story is so valuable—because it's real, it's raw, and it's relatable.

You see, people don't just buy coaching; they buy stories. They buy connections. They buy a piece of the journey that tells them, "If they made it, so can I." Your story isn't just a random collection of events; it's a strategic asset. It's the bridge that connects you to the hearts of those you are called to serve. And in this world where people are constantly bombarded with information, ads, and pitches, what stands out is not what you sell but the **story you tell**.

44

When I was starting my journey as a coach and a business leader, I thought I had to be perfect. I thought people wanted to see the highlight reel—only the wins, only the successes. But the more I shared the messy parts, the struggles, the setbacks, the losses—those were the moments that resonated most. Those were the moments when people leaned in and said, "That's my story too."

Take a look at the Bible for a second. The stories that we remember, the ones that inspire us, they're not about people who had it all together. They're about flawed, broken individuals who dared to trust God through their mess. David, a man after God's own heart, was also a man who made some serious mistakes. Yet, it was his raw authenticity—his highs and his lows—that connected with people. It's the same with you. Your story—every bit of it—holds value because it shows people that transformation is possible.

Here's why your story is so powerful in turning a potential sale into a yes:

Relatability: When people hear your story, they see themselves in it. They see their struggles, fears, and hopes reflected in them, and that creates a bond.

Credibility: Sharing your journey—the highs and the lows—builds trust. It shows that you've been in the trenches, and you've come out on the other side.

People don't want to follow perfection; they want to follow progress.

Emotion: People make decisions based on emotion first, then justify them with logic. Your story can touch hearts and stir emotions in a way that facts and figures never will.

So, what's the takeaway here? Don't shy away from your story. Don't hide the messy parts. They carry the keys to connecting with your audience and turning prospects into clients. Your story is your superpower.

How To Connect with Your Client by Using Your Story

Now that you understand the value of your story, let's talk about how to use it to connect with your clients. Connection is the foundation of any coaching relationship. Without it, you're just another voice in a sea of noise.

But when you master the art of storytelling, you create an unbreakable bond that draws clients to you like a magnet.

Here's the key to connecting with your clients using your story:

Vulnerability and Authenticity.

People can sense when you're being real and when you're putting on a front. They can tell when you're sharing from a place of genuine experience versus trying to be "relatable." Authenticity isn't about oversharing or airing out all your dirty laundry. It's about being honest about your journey and the lessons you've learned.

When I first started my coaching business, I tried to present myself as the guy who had all the answers. I thought that's what people wanted. But I quickly learned that nobody resonates with perfection. What people really wanted to hear was the story of a man who was just like them—someone who faced challenges, experienced setbacks, and found a way to rise above them.

Here are five samples of my story to illustrate how to connect with your clients:

The Story of My First Job: At 13, I was desperate for my first job. I remember the day I walked into Demperio's Market, a little chubby kid asking for a chance to stock shelves. I got turned down because of my age, but I didn't give up. On my 13th birthday, I went back and asked again. This time, I got the job. But the work wasn't what I expected—it was tough, messy, and humbling. I learned that perseverance isn't about the outcome; it's about showing up again and again, even after being told "no." When I share this story with clients, it connects with them on a personal level. They see a young boy who wouldn't take no for an answer, and it inspires them to keep pushing forward in their journeys.

The Story of Failure with My Magazine: When I started 3V Magazine, I had big dreams. And for a while, it looked like those dreams were coming true. We were on TV, doing interviews, signing autographs—it felt like I was on top of the world. But that success was built on shaky ground. I made some bad decisions and trusted the wrong people, and before I knew it, everything came crashing down. I went from being a rising star to losing everything. When I share this story, I'm not just sharing a failure; I'm sharing a lesson about the importance of foundation, integrity, and trusting God through the mess.

The Story of My Achilles Tendon Rupture: I ruptured my Achilles tendon not once but twice, back-to-back. I went from being active and moving to being stuck in a bed, questioning everything. It was a dark time for me, both physically and emotionally. I felt like I'd lost my way, my momentum, my purpose. But it was in that place of stillness that God began to speak to me. He reminded me that my steps are ordered, even when I can't see the path. This story connects with clients who feel like they're in a season of waiting, of being stuck. It reminds them that God's plan is always in motion, even when we don't see it.

The Story of My Divorce and Becoming a Single Father: When my marriage ended, I was devastated. I felt like I had failed at one of the most important roles in my life. But I also knew I had a choice—I could stay in that place of hurt, or I could rise up and become the father my daughter needed. I chose to rise. And in that process, I learned more about myself, my faith, and my purpose than I ever had before. When I share this story with my clients, it resonates with those who are facing personal challenges and need to be reminded that there's always hope on the other side of pain.

The Story of Launching My Security Business: Starting a security business while making $9.15 an hour was not the "success" story anyone expected from me. People thought I was crazy for leaving behind everything I had built before. But I knew God was calling me to this new path. I stayed focused, kept my head down, and worked relentlessly. Years later, that business hit seven figures. When I share this story, it connects with clients who feel like they're starting from the bottom, who need a reminder that success doesn't happen overnight, but it does happen with faith, focus, and relentless work.

The common thread in all these stories is that they're real. They're not sugar-coated or dressed up to look pretty. They're raw and they're honest. And that's what connects with people.

When you share your story, focus on the transformation. What did you learn? How did you grow? How did it shape who you are today? Your audience doesn't need another polished, perfect story. They need authenticity. They need to know that you've walked through the fire, and you've come out stronger on the other side. They need to see themselves in your story.

How Potential Clients Will Buy Based on Connecting with Your Story

Now, let's get down to the bottom line: **people buy based on connection**. And nothing connects more deeply than a story that resonates. When a potential client hears your story and sees themselves in it, something powerful happens—they start to believe that if it worked for you, it can work for them too. That's when trust is built, and trust is the foundation of any purchase decision.

Here's how potential clients make buying decisions based on your story:

They See Themselves in Your Journey: When a client hears your story and recognizes themselves in it—whether it's your struggle with failure, your path to self-discovery, or your journey to success—they start to feel like you're speaking directly to them. They see that you understand their pain, their challenges, and their dreams. That sense of empathy and understanding creates a connection that is far stronger than any sales pitch.

They Believe in Your Solutions Because They Worked for You: Sharing your story isn't just about sharing your struggles; it's about sharing how you overcame them. When potential clients hear about the steps you took to move from where you were to where you are now, they begin to see the value in your solutions. They start to believe that if those solutions worked for you, they can work for them too. It's the reason why testimonials and case studies are so powerful— they provide social proof that your methods are effective.

They Trust You as a Guide and Mentor: People don't just want a coach; they want a guide. They want someone who has walked the path before them and who can show them the way. When you share your story, you position yourself as that guide. You become the person they trust to lead them through their challenges and toward their goals. Trust is the most valuable currency in business, and your story is the key to building it.

They Are Inspired to Take Action: A compelling story moves people to action. When potential clients hear your story and feel inspired by your journey, they're more likely to take the next step—whether that's booking a call, signing up for a program, or making a purchase. Inspiration leads to action, and action leads to sales.

They Feel Part of a Larger Narrative: People want to feel like they're part of something bigger than themselves. When you share your story and invite them into your journey, they feel like they're joining a movement, a community, a shared mission. That sense of belonging is powerful, and it's a key driver of loyalty and long-term client relationships.

Final Thoughts: Your Story is Your Greatest Asset

As we close out this chapter, I want you to remember this: **Your story is your greatest asset**. It's the most authentic, compelling, and powerful tool you have to connect with your clients, build trust, and drive sales. Don't be afraid to share it. Don't hold back the parts that feel messy or uncomfortable. Those are the parts that will resonate the most.

So, take a moment to reflect on your story. Write it down. Refine it. Practice telling it in a way that is authentic to you and compelling to your audience. And most importantly, use it to serve. Use it to inspire. Use it to transform. Your story has the power to change lives—including your own. Let's make it count.

"High-ticket sales aren't about hard selling; they're about deep understanding and genuine solutions."

Breakout Exercise

Storytelling Worksheet for Coaches: Crafting Your Story to Connect with Clients

Instructions: This worksheet is designed to help you, as a coach, craft a compelling story that resonates with your ideal clients, builds trust, and inspires them to take action. Follow each section carefully and take your time reflecting on each question to develop a powerful narrative that truly connects.

Discovering the Core of Your Story

1. Identify Your Pivotal Moments

Think about the key moments in your life and career that have shaped who you are today. These are the turning points, the challenges, the triumphs, and the failures that have led you to become a coach. List at least three pivotal moments below:

Pivotal Moment #1:
What happened?

_____

_____

_____

How did this moment challenge or change you?

_____

_____

_____

What lesson did you learn from this experience?

_____

_____

_____

Pivotal Moment #2:
  What happened?

_____

_____

_____

  How did this moment challenge or change you?

_____

_____

_____

  What lesson did you learn from this experience?

_____

_____

_____

Pivotal Moment #3:

How did this moment challenge or change you?

_____

_____

_____

What lesson did you learn from this experience?

_____

_____

_____

2. Define Your Transformation Journey

Your clients need to see the journey you've been on and how you've transformed because of it. This gives them hope that they can achieve their transformation too.

Where were you before your transformation?
(Describe the mindset, situation, or problem you were facing.)

_____

_____

_____

What was the catalyst for change?
(What was the event, realization, or experience that pushed you to)

_____

_____

_____

_____

How did you navigate the change?
(What actions did you take? What resources did you use? Who helped you along the way?)

_____

_____

_____

Where are you now?
(Describe the mindset, situation, or achievements you have now because of your journey.)

_____

_____

_____

3. Understand Your Audience's Pain Points and Desires
To connect with your clients, your story needs to resonate with their experiences, struggles, and aspirations. Reflect on your ideal client's current state and what they desire most.

What are the three biggest points of pain or challenges your ideal clients face?

1

_____

_____

2

_____

_____

3

_____

_____

What are the top three desires or goals of your ideal clients?

1

_____

_____

_____

2

_____

_____

_____

3

_____

_____

_____

4. Find the Overlap Between Your Story and Your Client's Needs

Think about how your journey and transformation align with your client's needs. Write down how each pivotal moment or lesson you've learned can help solve their problems or achieve their desires.

Pivotal Moment #1 Connection:
How does this moment resonate with what your clients are going through?

_____

_____

_____

Pivotal Moment #2 Connection:
How does this moment resonate with what your clients are going through?

_____

_____

_____

Pivotal Moment #3 Connection:
How does this moment resonate with what your clients are going through?

_____

_____

_____

Crafting and Telling Your Story

5. Create a Compelling Story Structure
Use the classic "Hero's Journey" structure to tell your story in a way that engages your audience:

Introduction:

Briefly introduce yourself and your "before" state (the struggle).

_____

_____

_____

Conflict:

Describe the challenges or problems you faced. Be specific and relatable. This is where you connect emotionally with your audience.

_____

_____

_____

Turning Point:

Share the moment of change or realization. What was the catalyst that pushed you to take action?

_____

Action:

What steps did you take to overcome your challenges? Share your process, the tools you used, and the help you sought.

_____

_____

_____

Resolution:

Describe where you are now, your achievements, and how you have transformed.

_____

_____

_____

_____

Call to Action:

Invite your audience to take the next step with you. Whether it's booking a call, signing up for a program, or following you on social media, be clear about what you want them to do.

_____

_____

_____

_____

Draft Your Story Using the Story Structure

Use the space below to draft your story using the structure above. Don't worry about perfection—focus on getting your thoughts down.

Introduction:

_____

_____

_____

Conflict:

_____

_____

_____

Turning Point:

_____

_____

_____

Action:

_____

_____

_____

Resolution:

_____

_____

_____

Call to Action:

_____

_____

_____

Refine Your Story for Authenticity and Impact

Now that you have a draft, review your story for the following:

Authenticity:

Are you being honest and vulnerable? Are you sharing the real challenges and emotions you experienced?

_____

_____

_____

Relatability:

Will your audience see themselves in your story? Are you using language and examples that are relevant to them?

_____

_____

_____

Brevity:

Is your story concise and to the point? Make sure every part of your story adds value and keeps your audience engaged.

_____

_____

_____

Impact:

Does your story inspire action? Are you guiding your audience towards a clear next step?

_____

_____

_____

Practice Telling Your Story

Practice sharing your story with a friend, colleague, or mentor. Get feedback on what resonates and what can be improved. Remember, storytelling is an art that gets better with practice. The more you tell your story, the more natural and impactful it will become.

Feedback Notes:
What parts of your story resonated most with your listener?

What suggestions did they provide for improvement?

Incorporate Your Story into Your Marketing

Think about how you can weave your story into different aspects of your marketing:

Social Media Posts: Write a series of posts that share snippets of your story.

About Me Page: Make sure your website reflects your journey and transformation.

Emails: Use your story to connect with your email subscribers and provide value.

Webinars/Workshops: Start with your story to build rapport and trust with your audience.

Review and Revisit Your Story Regularly

Your story will evolve as you grow and learn. Make it a habit to revisit your story every few months to see if there are new insights, experiences, or transformations that should be included.

_____

_____

_____

_____

_____

_____

_____

_____

_____

_____

_____

_____

"Coaching isn't about teaching; it's about unlocking what's already inside your client."

Chapter 5: Build Your Premium Coaching Brand

If you're going to make it in this coaching game, you've got to have more than just a good offer or some nice packaging. You've got to build a brand. Not just any brand, but a premium coaching brand that sets you apart from the sea of sameness out there. You see, in a world where anyone can put up a website, call themselves a coach, and start offering services, what will set you apart? What will make people stop, look, and say, "I need to work with them"? It all comes down to **your brand**.

What Exactly is a Brand? Unlocking the Mystery and Confusion
Let's cut through the confusion right here, right now. When most people think of a brand, they think of logos, colors, or maybe a catchy tagline. And while those things are elements of a brand, they are not the brand itself. A **brand** is so much deeper than that. It's the promise you make to your audience. It's the experience people have when they interact with you or your business. It's what people say about you when you're not in the room.

A brand is the emotional connection that people feel when they think about you or your business. It's the sum of perceptions—how you make people feel, the value you bring, the impact you create, and the story you tell. Your brand is the intangible essence that creates loyalty, drives trust, and ultimately influences purchasing decisions.

Think of a brand as a **relationship**. When you build a brand, you're not just building a business; you're building a relationship with your audience. And just like any relationship, it takes time, consistency, and authenticity to build something that lasts.

Here's a simple way to think about it: **A brand is not what you say it is; it's what they say it is.** You can talk all day long about what you want your brand to be, but the real question is—what do people actually feel and think when they interact with you? That's your brand.

Why Are People Drawn to Brands?

To understand why people are drawn to certain brands, let's break down a few powerful examples: **Apple, Gucci, and the Jay-Z brand**. Each of these brands tells a story, creates an emotion, and offers a status that people desire. Let's dive deep into what makes these brands tick and why people gravitate toward them.

Apple
Established: 1976
Founders: Steve Jobs, Steve Wozniak, and Ronald Wayne
Ownership: Publicly traded company (AAPL)

Apple is not just a company that makes phones, computers, or tablets. Apple is a lifestyle. It's a status symbol. When people buy an Apple product, they're not just buying a piece of technology; they're buying a piece of the Apple ecosystem—a sleek, sophisticated world that promises innovation, simplicity, and premium quality. Apple's brand is built on the idea of thinking differently. From the very beginning, Apple positioned itself as a disruptor, a brand for the creative, the innovators, and the game-changers. When you buy an Apple product, you're telling the world that you're part of that tribe. You're saying, "I'm a visionary. I value innovation."

Apple's branding is about more than just their product's sleek design and user friendly interface. It's about the **experience**—the feeling of unboxing a new iPhone or MacBook, the elegance of their retail stores, and the seamless integration of their ecosystem. When people buy Apple, they feel like they're buying into a premium, exclusive club.

Gucci
Established: 1921
Founder: Guccio Gucci
Ownership: Kering (a luxury group company)

Gucci is the epitome of luxury, elegance, and high fashion. When people think of Gucci, they think of status, sophistication, and a certain level of exclusivity. This Italian fashion house has built its brand on being a symbol of wealth and refined taste. It's not just about the clothes or accessories; it's about the **story** that comes with wearing Gucci. It says, "I have arrived. I'm successful. I know quality."

Gucci has masterfully cultivated a sense of rarity and prestige around its products. Whether it's the iconic GG logo, the timeless handbags, or the unique runway collections, Gucci communicates that owning a piece of their brand is owning a piece of luxury history. It's not just fashion—it's a lifestyle statement. When people buy Gucci, they are buying status, and they want to be identified with that level of luxury and refinement.

Jay-Z Brand
Established: Late 1990s
Founder: Shawn "Jay-Z" Carter
Ownership: Jay-Z

Jay-Z, one of the most successful entrepreneurs and artists of our time, has turned his name into a brand that represents success, hustle, and the ultimate "come up" story. The Jay-Z brand isn't just about music; it's about business acumen, cultural influence, and defying the odds. Jay-Z has branded himself as someone who came from humble beginnings and built an empire—music, fashion, liquor, sports, and streaming services. When people buy into the Jay-Z brand, they're buying into the idea that they too can hustle, build, and achieve.

People gravitate toward the Jay-Z brand because it represents the **American Dream**—a relentless pursuit of success and influence. It's aspirational. Jay-Z's fans don't just listen to his music or buy his products; they follow his moves, study his investments, and see him as a blueprint for success.

People buy these brands not just for the products but for what they represent. **They buy because they want to be identified with that brand.** They want to feel like they are part of a community, a movement, a status. They want to say, "I'm an Apple person," "I wear Gucci," or "I'm inspired by Jay-Z's hustle."

A powerful brand doesn't just sell products or services; it sells a story. It creates a narrative that draws people in and makes them feel something. The story behind a brand is what gives it life, personality, and emotional connection. And here's the kicker: **People remember stories, not statistics.** If you want to build a premium coaching brand, you have to understand how to weave your story into the fabric of your brand.

Let's go back to our examples:

Apple's Story: From a garage in California to becoming one of the most valuable companies in the world, Apple's story is one of innovation, disruption, and simplicity. The "Think Different" campaign wasn't just a tagline; it was a rallying cry for the misfits, the rebels, and the creatives who wanted to change the world. Apple tells a story of challenging the status quo, and every product they release is a chapter in that ongoing narrative.

Gucci's Story: Gucci's story is deeply rooted in Italian craftsmanship, luxury, and heritage. It tells the story of a brand that has stood the test of time by adapting to the changing world while staying true to its roots. From being a small leather goods shop in Florence to becoming a global fashion powerhouse, Gucci's story is one of elegance, exclusivity, and timeless style.

Jay-Z's Story: Jay-Z's brand story is a modern-day saga of the "hustler's ambition." It's about rising from the Marcy Projects in Brooklyn to building a billion dollar empire. His story connects with people who value grit, determination, and strategic moves. Jay-Z's brand is about breaking barriers, and his story resonates with anyone who has ever been told they couldn't achieve something and then went on to prove them wrong.

When you understand the power of storytelling in branding, you realize that you are not just selling coaching services—you are selling a vision, a transformation, and a narrative that your clients want to be a part of. **Your story and your brand must be intertwined.** They should be inseparable. When people think of your brand, they should think of your story and vice versa.

Comparisons to draw perspective

Now, let's draw some comparisons between brands that may appeal to different audiences. Think about **Kenneth Cole vs. Gucci**. Both are fashion brands, but they represent very different stories and attract different consumers.

Kenneth Cole: Established in 1982, Kenneth Cole is known for its stylish, modern, and practical designs that cater to a more accessible market. The brand emphasizes functionality, affordability, and social consciousness. Kenneth Cole has been vocal about various social causes, which appeals to a more socially aware audience. People who buy Kenneth Cole might be looking for style without the hefty price tag, and they may be motivated by the brand's stance on social issues.

Gucci: On the other hand, Gucci represents the pinnacle of luxury, exclusivity, and high fashion. It is a status symbol. People who buy Gucci are often looking for a statement piece, something that exudes wealth, style, and an appreciation for high-end fashion.

So, why might a consumer choose Kenneth Cole over Gucci, or vice versa? It comes down to what they value. If they value exclusivity, prestige, and high fashion, they'll gravitate towards Gucci. If they value style, practicality, and social awareness, they might choose Kenneth Cole.

The same principle applies when comparing the Jay-Z Brand and Celine Dion's Brand:

Jay-Z Brand: Represents the hustle, the grind, and the story of turning nothing into something. It's a brand for those who see themselves as entrepreneurs, visionaries, and game-changers.

Celine Dion's Brand: Represents elegance, vocal excellence, and timeless music. It appeals to those who appreciate the classic, the refined, and the sophisticated.

Each brand tells a different story, and each attracts a different type of consumer based on the narrative they connect with.

How to Build a Premium Brand That Draws Attraction

So, how do you build a premium coaching brand that draws attraction? It starts with understanding that a brand is more than a logo, a tagline, or a product. It's about the experience, the promise, and the story you deliver consistently to your audience. Here are five key questions to consider when building your premium attraction brand:

What is Your Brand Story?

What are the key moments, lessons, and experiences that have shaped who you are as a coach? How do these stories align with the values and desires of your ideal clients?

What Emotional Experience Do You Want Your Brand to Create?

How do you want people to feel when they interact with your brand? Inspired, motivated, safe, challenged? Define the emotional experience you want to deliver and build everything around that.

What Makes Your Brand Unique?

What sets you apart from other coaches in your niche? What is the unique promise of value that only you can deliver? Is it your approach, your story, your method, or your personality?

Who Is Your Ideal Client?

Who are you building this brand for? What are their pain points, desires, and aspirations? Your brand should speak directly to the people you are called to serve.

What Consistent Message Do You Want to Communicate?

Your brand is not just a one-time story; it's a consistent message that you communicate across every touchpoint—your website, social media, email, workshops, and more. What message do you want people to remember?

Here are 5 samples of how I've built my own brand:

Authenticity and Transparency: My brand is built on sharing my real-life experiences, both the successes and the failures. I'm not afraid to show the messy parts because that's where the real connection happens.

Faith-Driven Purpose: My brand is unapologetically faith-driven. I make it clear that my coaching is not just about business—it's about aligning with God's purpose for your life.

Relentless Focus on Results: My brand is focused on helping clients get real results. I emphasize strategy, execution, and accountability because that's what drives transformation.

Empowering Community: I've built a community around my brand that's focused on support, growth, and shared success. My clients don't just get me; they get access to a network of like-minded individuals who are on the same journey.

Bold, No-Nonsense Messaging: My brand voice is bold, direct, and no nonsense. I'm here to challenge my clients, push them out of their comfort zones, and help them achieve what they never thought possible.

Final Thoughts:

Building Your Premium Coaching Brand

Your brand is not just a logo or a tagline. It's the promise you make to your clients, the story you tell, and the experience you deliver. When you build a premium brand, you're not just creating a business—you're creating a movement, a community, a legacy. So, take the time to craft it well. Be intentional, be authentic, and be relentless in delivering value. Because when you do, your brand will not just attract clients; it will create raving fans who are proud to be part of your journey. Your premium coaching brand starts with you. Let's build it, one powerful story at a time.

"Your value isn't in what you sell; it's in the transformation you deliver."

__Breakout Exercise__

The Brand Strategy of Jay-Z: A Step-by-Step Worksheet for Coaches:

Jay-Z has masterfully built a brand that transcends music, becoming a symbol of success, innovation, and influence. His brand is rooted in authenticity, strategic moves, and a deep connection with his audience. As a coach, you can apply similar principles to build your own powerful brand. This worksheet will guide you through the process, using in-depth techniques that mirror the strategies behind Jay-Z's brand.

Define Your Brand Identity

Jay-Z's brand identity is built on the foundation of his personal story, his values, and his unique perspective. To build your brand, start by defining your own brand identity.

Clarify Your Core Values:

Jay-Z's brand is rooted in values like hustle, authenticity, and innovation. What are the core values that drive you and your coaching business?

Core Value #1:

_____

Core Value #2:

_____

Core Value #3:

_____

Your Mission Statement:

Jay-Z's mission has evolved from dominating the rap game to empowering others through business and culture. What is the mission of your brand? What impact do you want to have?

Mission Statement:

_____

_____

_____

_____

_____

Define Your Unique Voice:

Jay-Z's voice is bold, confident, and unapologetic. What tone and style do you want your brand to convey? How do you want to be perceived?

Voice and Tone:

_____

_____

_____

_____

Articulate Your Brand Story:

Jay-Z's brand story includes his rise from the Marcy Projects to becoming a global business mogul. Your brand story should highlight your journey, your challenges, and your transformation.

Brand Story:

_____

_____

_____

_____

_____

_____

_____

_____

_____

Build Brand Credibility and Trust

Jay-Z built credibility through consistency, quality, and strategic partnerships. To build your brand's credibility, focus on the following areas:

Showcase Your Expertise:

Jay-Z established himself as a leader in his field before expanding his brand. How will you showcase your expertise in your niche? (e.g., writing a book, speaking engagements, client testimonials)

Expertise Showcases:

_____

_____

_____

_____

Leverage Strategic Partnerships:

Jay-Z strategically aligned himself with brands like Rocawear, Armand de Brignac, and Tidal. Who can you partner with to elevate your brand?

Potential Strategic Partners:

_____

_____

_____

_____

Consistently Deliver Quality:

Jay-Z's brand is synonymous with high-quality music, fashion, and business ventures. How will you ensure that your brand consistently delivers high-quality experiences for your clients?

Quality Assurance Plan:

_____

_____

Build Social Proof:

Jay-Z's brand is backed by awards, endorsements, and public recognition. How will you build social proof for your brand? (e.g., client testimonials, industry awards, media features)

Social Proof Strategies:

_____

_____

Create a Strong Visual Identity

Jay-Z's brand is visually represented through his music videos, album covers, and fashion lines. A strong visual identity will make your brand recognizable and memorable.

Develop a Logo and Brand Colors:

Jay-Z's logos, such as the Roc Nation symbol, are iconic. What will your logo and brand colors represent? How do they align with your brand values and mission?

Logo Concept:

_____

_____

Brand Colors:

_____

_____

Design a Professional Website:

Jay-Z's online presence, including his website and social media, is sleek and professional. What key elements will your website include to reflect your brand?

Website Elements:

_____

_____

_____

_____

_____

_____

_____

_____

_____

Curate Your Social Media Presence:

Jay-Z uses social media to reinforce his brand's message and connect with his audience. How will you create your social media profiles to reflect your brand?

    Social Media Strategy:

_____

_____

_____

_____

_____

_____

_____

_____

_____

_____

_____

_____

_____

_____

Connect Deeply with Your Audience

Jay-Z's connection with his audience is rooted in authenticity, relatability, and understanding of their needs. To connect deeply with your audience, focus on these techniques:

Understand Your Audience:

Jay-Z knows his audience and speaks directly to their experiences. Who is your target audience, and what are their pain points, desires, and needs?

Audience Profile:

_____

_____

Engage with Authentic Content:

Jay-Z shares his life experiences and wisdom through his music and interviews. What authentic content can you create to engage your audience? (e.g., blog posts, videos, podcasts)

Content Ideas:

_____

_____

Offer Value and Solutions:

Jay-Z offers value through his lyrics, business ventures, and philanthropy. How will you offer value to your audience and solve their problems?

Value Offerings:

_____

_____

_____

_____

_____

_____

_____

_____

_____

_____

_____

_____

Build a community:

Jay-Z's fan base is loyal because they feel connected to him and his story. How will you build a community around your brand? (e.g., Facebook groups, live events, webinars)

Community Building Plan:

_____

_____

_____

Expand and Diversify Your Brand

Jay-Z didn't stop at music—he expanded into fashion, streaming services, and sports management. To build a brand with staying power, consider how you can expand and diversify.

Identifying New Opportunities:

What new products, services, or markets could you expand into that align with your brand?

Expansion Opportunities:

_____

_____

_____

_____

Innovate and Adapt:

Jay-Z has consistently evolved his brand to stay relevant. How will you innovate and adapt your brand to changing trends and audience needs?

Innovation Strategies:

Scale Your Brand:

Jay-Z scaled his brand through strategic partnerships and investments. How will you scale your brand for growth? (e.g., online courses, group coaching, franchising)

_____

_____

_____

_____

_____

_____

Final Reflection: Integrating Jay-Z's Branding Techniques into Your Coaching Business

As you complete this worksheet, reflect on how you can integrate the in-depth branding techniques used by Jay-Z into your own coaching business. What are the key takeaways that will shape your brand's future?

Key Takeaways:

Use this worksheet as a roadmap to build a brand that not only reflects who you are but also resonates deeply with your audience, much like Jay-Z's brand has done over the years. Your brand has the potential to become a powerful force in the coaching industry—one that inspires, influences, and leaves a lasting impact.

"To stand out, you must first stand firm in who you are and what you believe."

Chapter 6:
Cashflow Revenue
Generation Strategy

Coaches, if there's one thing I've learned over the years, it's that a thriving coaching business isn't built on hope, hype, or happenstance—it's built on a solid strategy for generating cash flow. And not just any cash flow, but consistent, predictable, and scalable cash flow that allows you to not only survive but thrive in your business. This chapter is about laying out that strategy—based on the Value Ladder concept championed by Russell Brunson, combined with the brilliance of Myron Golden's approach to offer creation. Buckle up, because we're about to dive deep into crafting a revenue-generation strategy that will change the game for your coaching business.

Understanding the Value Ladder

The Value Ladder is a powerful concept that was introduced. The idea behind the Value Ladder is simple: you start by offering something of value at a low price point to attract clients, and as they gain trust and see the value in what you offer, they move up the ladder to higher-priced, more value-packed offers. This progression allows you to build a relationship with your clients, solve their problems incrementally, and increase the lifetime value of each client.

Here's a breakdown of how the Value Ladder works:

Entry-Level Offer (Low Ticket): This is where you provide a high value offer at a low cost to bring new clients into your ecosystem. Think of it as a way to start the relationship. For example, a $14.99 book or a $27 mini course that provides immediate value.

Mid-Tier Offer (Middle Ticket): As clients begin to see the value you provide, they're more likely to invest in a slightly higher-priced offer, such as a group coaching session, a masterclass, or an online workshop. These offers are typically in the $97 to $297 range and dive deeper into solving specific pain points.

Recurring Revenue Offer (Subscription Model): This is the sweet spot for consistent cash flow. A subscription model or membership program offers ongoing value, such as monthly coaching calls, exclusive content, or access to a community, for a regular fee. Pricing here can range from $47 to $297 per month.

High-Ticket Offer (Premium): Once clients have experienced the value of your lower and mid-tier offers, they may be ready for a more substantial investment. This could be one-on-one coaching, a multi-day workshop, or a deep-dive program. These premium offers typically range from $1,997 to $10,000 or more.

Mastermind Offer (Elite): You offer a high-value mastermind program for your most committed clients. This is where the real transformation happens.

Masterminds provide direct access to you, as well as a group of high-level peers who are committed to growth. These programs can range from $10,000 to $50,000 or more.

The key to the Value Ladder is progression. You don't ask someone to invest $10,000 the first time they meet you. You start small, build trust, deliver massive value, and then ascend them through your offers as they become more engaged and committed to their transformation.

Crafting Your Value Ladder Offers

Now, let's break down each step of the Value Ladder and explore how you can implement it in your coaching business. I'm also going to share how I've used each of these models to grow my coaching practice and how I teach my clients to do the same.

1. Entry-Level Offer: The $14.99 Book or $27 Mini-Course

Purpose: The purpose of the entry-level offer is simple: get clients into your ecosystem. This offer should provide high value and solve a specific problem that your ideal client is facing. Think of it as the "lead magnet" that attracts clients and gets them invested in your coaching journey.

Pricing Range: $14.99 - $27

Example: A book that outlines foundational principles or a mini course that offers a quick win. For instance, I offer a book called *"Fortify Your Mindset: The Foundation for Coaching Success,"* priced at $14.99. It's packed with strategies, actionable steps, and stories that help potential clients see immediate results. This entry-level offer builds trust and positions me as an authority.

How to Implement: Create a high-value, low-cost product that addresses a pain point for your ideal client. Use platforms like Amazon Kindle, Gumroad, or your website to sell your entry level offer. Leverage social media, email marketing, and ads to promote this offer and attract new clients.

Teaching My Clients: I advise my coaching clients to focus on one core pain point that their ideal client is struggling with. Develop an entry-level offer that addresses that pain point and provides an immediate solution. This is your gateway to building a relationship.

2. Mid-Tier Offer: Group Webinar, Masterclass, or Workshop

Purpose: The mid-tier offer allows you to go deeper with your clients and provide more personalized value. This offer is where you start to create a more profound transformation by providing interactive and hands-on coaching.

Pricing Range: $97 - $297

Example: A 3-hour masterclass on *"Building Your Premium Coaching Brand,"* priced at $197, where I teach clients the step-by-step process of defining their brand, creating an emotional connection with their audience, and leveraging it for growth. The masterclass includes live Q&A, worksheets, and personalized feedback.

How to Implement:
Choose a specific topic that your audience wants to learn more about. This should be a natural extension of your entry-level offer. Host live webinars or masterclasses via platforms like Zoom or Webinar Jam. Record these sessions and offer them as evergreen content for ongoing sales.

Teaching My Clients: I tell my clients that their mid-tier offer should be an "experience," not just a transaction. This is where you start to build community, engage with clients directly, and begin to create a loyal following.

3. Recurring Revenue Offer: Membership or Subscription Model

Purpose: Recurring revenue models are the backbone of a sustainable coaching business. The goal here is to provide continuous value and keep clients engaged over the long term.

Pricing Range: $47 - $297 per month

Example: I offer a subscription-based coaching community called the *"Suber Success Circle,"* priced at $97 per month. Members get access to monthly coaching calls, exclusive content, guest expert sessions, and a private community forum. The recurring revenue allows me to maintain a steady cash flow while continuously nurturing my clients.

How to Implement:
Develop a membership program that offers ongoing value. This could include monthly coaching calls, new content, resources, templates, and access to a community. Use platforms like Kajabi, Teachable, or Patreon to host your membership site. Focus on retention by consistently delivering value and engaging with your members.

Teaching My Clients: I emphasize the importance of having a recurring revenue model as it provides financial stability and predictability. I teach them how to create compelling offers that keep members subscribed for the long term by continuously delivering value and building a sense of community.

4. High-Ticket Offer: One-on-One Coaching or Intensive Programs

Purpose: The high-ticket offer is where you provide a personalized, transformative experience for your clients. This is for those who are ready to invest significantly in their growth and want direct access to your expertise.

Pricing Range: $1,997 - $10,000+

Example: My *"Executive Coaching Program"* is a high-ticket offer priced at $7,500 for six months of intensive one-on-one coaching. This program is tailored to high performing professionals and business owners looking to scale their businesses while maintaining balance in other areas of life.

How to Implement: Create a high-ticket offer that provides in-depth transformation, personalized coaching, and direct access to you. Develop a comprehensive curriculum or program that takes clients through a step-by-step process. Use sales calls, webinars, and email marketing to promote and sell this offer.

Teaching My Clients: I teach my clients to be confident in their high-ticket offers. I remind them that people pay for results, not time. If you can help someone achieve a massive transformation, don't be afraid to price your services accordingly.

5. Mastermind Offer: The Ultimate Elite Offer

Purpose: Masterminds are for your most committed clients who want a combination of personal coaching, group support, and high-level networking. This is where the real game-changers play, and it's an incredible way to build long-term client relationships.

Pricing Range: $10,000 - $50,000+

Example: I run a *"High-Impact Leaders Mastermind,"* an elite group for top-level entrepreneurs and business owners. Priced at $25,000 per year, this mastermind provides monthly in-person retreats, bi-weekly group calls, access to guest experts, and exclusive networking opportunities. Clients who join this group are looking to scale significantly and surround themselves with like-minded achievers.

How to Implement: Curate a small, exclusive group of high-performing clients who are committed to growth. Offer a combination of in-person and virtual events, mastermind sessions, hot seats, and peer support. Focus on creating a high-value experience that justifies the price point.

Teaching My Clients: I help my clients understand that masterminds are more than just group coaching—they are a space for transformation, collaboration, and high-level networking. I teach them to build their mastermind around specific outcomes and create an environment where members feel they are getting 10x the value of their investment.

The Importance of Recurring Revenue in Coaching

Let's get something straight—if you want to build a sustainable coaching business, you cannot rely solely on one-time sales. Recurring revenue is the key to creating financial stability, enabling you to plan for growth, hire team members, and invest back into your business.

Why Recurring Revenue Matters

Predictability: Recurring revenue allows you to forecast income, manage cash flow, and make strategic decisions with confidence.

Client Retention: A subscription model keeps clients engaged and builds loyalty. The longer they stay, the more value they get, and the more likely they are to ascend the Value Ladder.

Scalability: With a recurring model, you can scale your impact without having to constantly find new clients. Focus on retention and providing consistent value.

How I Teach Recurring Revenue to My Clients:
I encourage my clients to think beyond one-off transactions and build a recurring revenue model from the ground up. Whether it's a membership site, subscription-based coaching, or a continuity program, the focus should always be on delivering ongoing value that keeps clients engaged and coming back for more.

Deep Diving into Offer Creation Techniques

A mentor of mine is a master at creating irresistible offers that sell themselves. He emphasizes the importance of understanding your client's true desires and crafting offers that are perceived as "insane value."

Key Principles:

Stack the Value: Your offers should feel like a steal compared to the price. If a client pays $297 for a subscription, they should feel like they're getting $2,970 worth of value.

Solve a Specific Problem: Each offer should be laser-focused on solving a specific problem your client is facing. The more specific, the more valuable.

Make it Simple to Understand: The more complex the offer, the harder it is to sell. Make sure your offers are simple, clear, and easy to understand.

Create Urgency and Scarcity: People are more likely to take action when they feel like they're missing out. Use limited-time offers, bonuses, and scarcity tactics to encourage conversions.

Applying These Techniques in Your Coaching Business:

Entry-Level Offer Example: A "$14.99 Book + 3 Free Bonuses" deal. Stack the value by including a workbook, an audio version, and a free coaching call.

Mid-Tier Offer Example: A "$197 Masterclass" with a "$2,000 Value" bonus bundle—templates, checklists, and scripts to implement immediately.

Recurring Revenue Offer Example: A "$97/month Membership" with a free "30day trial" to reduce risk and encourage sign-ups.

High-Ticket Offer Example: A "$5,000 One-on-One Coaching Program" with a "$10,000 Guarantee"—if they don't see results in six months, they get double their investment back.

Final Thoughts: Implementing the Cashflow Revenue Generation Strategy

Building a coaching business that thrives is all about implementing a smart cash flow strategy that allows you to serve more clients, deliver more value, and create financial stability. The Value Ladder, combined with recurring revenue models and high-ticket offers, provides a comprehensive blueprint to achieve this.

Remember, the goal is to create a journey for your clients—a journey that starts with a small commitment and grows into a life-changing experience. Every step up the ladder should build on the previous one, creating more value, more connection, and more impact. Start building your Value Ladder today, and watch how it transforms not only your coaching business but the lives of the clients you're called to serve.

"The quickest way to elevate your brand is to serve relentlessly and add value unapologetically."

Breakout Exercise

Value Ladder Development Worksheet for Coaches

Instructions: This worksheet is designed to help you, as a coach, develop a comprehensive Value Ladder using Offer Creation techniques. Follow each section carefully and fill in the blanks to build a structured revenue strategy that guides clients from entry-level offers to premium, high-ticket services.

Define Your Value Ladder

The Value Ladder is about creating a series of offers that gradually increase in value and price. This allows your clients to move through your coaching programs, starting with an entry-level offer and ascending to your most premium service.

Step 1: Entry-Level Offer

Purpose: Attract potential clients into your ecosystem by providing high value at a low cost. Solve a specific pain point or provide a quick win.

Offer Type (e.g., Book, Mini-Course):

_____

_____

Offer Description:

_____

_____

_____

Pricing ($14.99):

_____

_____

_____

What Pain Point Does This Solve?

_____

_____

_____

_____

How Will You Promote This Offer? (e.g., Social media, Ads, Email Marketing):

_____

_____

_____

_____

Step 2: Mid-Tier Offer

Purpose: Provide more in-depth value and establish a stronger connection with clients. This offer should expand on the entry-level offer and provide more comprehensive solutions.

Offer Type (e.g., Group Webinar, Masterclass, Workshop):
Offer Description:

_____

_____

_____

_____

_____

_____

Pricing ($97 - $297):

_____

_____

_____

What Additional Value Does This Offer Provide?

_____

_____

_____

_____

_____

How Will You Deliver This Offer? (e.g., Live Sessions, Recorded Content):

_____

_____

_____

Step 3: Recurring Revenue Offer

Purpose: Establish a consistent revenue stream by offering continuous value through a membership or subscription model.

Offer Type (e.g., Membership, Subscription-Based Program):

Offer Description:

_____

_____

_____

Pricing ($297 - $497):

_____

_____

_____

What Ongoing Value Will You Provide? (e.g., Monthly Coaching,

_____

_____

How Will You Keep Clients Engaged and Subscribed Long-Term?

(Exclusive Content):

_____

Step 4: High-Ticket Offer

Purpose: Deliver a transformative experience through personalized, high impact coaching or intensive programs.

Offer Type (e.g., One-on-One Coaching, Intensive Program):

_____

_____

_____

Offer Description:

_____

_____

Pricing ($1,997 - $10,000+):

_____

_____

What Transformation or Result Will This Offer Provide?

_____

_____

How Will You Sell This Offer? (e.g., Sales Calls, Webinars, Email Funnels):

_____

_____

Step 5: Mastermind Offer

Purpose: Offer exclusive access to you and a network of high-achieving peers for deep transformation and advanced growth.

Offer Type (e.g., Mastermind Group, Elite Retreat): Offer Description: Pricing ($10,000 - $50,000+):

_____

_____

What Makes This Offer Exclusive and High-Value?

_____

_____

_____

What Is the Main Outcome Clients Will Achieve Through This   Offer?

_____

_____

_____

Crafting Irresistible Offers Using Myron Golden's Techniques

Myron Golden's offer creation techniques focus on maximizing perceived value
and delivering irresistible offers that solve specific problems.

1. Stack the Value

How Can You Stack the Value in Each Offer? (List Bonuses, Extras, or Addons for Each Offer) **Entry-Level Offer Bonuses:**

_____

_____

_____

Mid-Tier Offer Bonuses:

_____

_____

_____

Recurring Revenue Offer Bonuses:

_____

_____

_____

High-Ticket Offer Bonuses: Mastermind Offer Bonuses:

_____

_____

_____

2. Create Urgency and Scarcity

What Elements Will You Use to Create Urgency for Each Offer?
(e.g., Limited-Time Discount, only 10 Spots Available)

Entry-Level Offer Urgency Tactic:

_____

_____

_____

_____

Mid-Tier Offer Urgency Tactic:

_____

_____

_____

Recurring Revenue Offer Urgency Tactic:

_____

_____

High-Ticket Offer Urgency Tactic:

_____

_____

_____

_____

Mastermind Offer Urgency Tactic:

_____

_____

_____

_____

3. Solving a Specific Problem

What Specific Problem Does Each Offer Solve?
Entry-Level Offer Problem Solved:

_____

_____

_____

Mid-Tier Offer Problem Solved:

_____

_____

_____

Recurring Revenue Offer Problem Solved:
High-Ticket Offer Problem Solved:

_____

_____

_____

Mastermind Offer Problem Solved:

_____

_____

4. Making Offers Simple to Understand

How Can You Simplify Each Offer to Make It Easy for Clients to Understand? Entry-Level Offer Simplicity Strategy:

_____

_____

Mid-Tier Offer Simplicity Strategy:

_____

_____

Recurring Revenue Offer Simplicity Strategy:

_____

_____

High-Ticket Offer Simplicity Strategy:

_____

_____

Mastermind Offer Simplicity Strategy:

_____

_____

Reflect and Optimize Your Value Ladder

What Are Your Key Takeaways After Building Your Value Ladder?

_____

_____

What Areas Need Further Refinement or Testing?

_____

_____

_____

How Will You Measure the Success of Each Offer on the Value Ladder?

_____

_____

_____

What Is Your Next Step to Implement and Launch Your Value Ladder?

_____

_____

_____

_____

_____

_____

_____

_____

_____

Final Thought:

Your Value Ladder is a dynamic, evolving strategy that should be refined and optimized based on client feedback and performance. Keep testing, learning, and adjusting to ensure you're delivering massive value at every step of your coaching journey. Let's build a Value Ladder that not only attracts clients but transforms lives and creates sustainable revenue for your business!

"Master your narrative, and you'll master your market."

Chapter 7: Building Your Dream Team: The Do's and Don'ts of Hiring Right

---

Introduction

Listen, when it comes to building a business that stands the test of time, the team you build is everything. As entrepreneurs, we all know this journey can be a lonely road, but it doesn't have to be. The people you bring on board—those you hire and choose to share your vision—are more than just employees. They are the foundation, the drivers, and the heartbeat of your mission. The right team will elevate your business; the wrong team can drag you down. In this chapter, we're going to break down the **do's and don'ts** of hiring in plain, no-nonsense terms. By following these principles, you can craft a team that not only fits but fuels your purpose.

The Do's of Hiring Right

Do Clearly Define Roles and Expectations

Here's the deal: Before you bring anyone into your business, you need to get clear—crystal clear—on what you want and need. That means creating job descriptions that outline not just the tasks, but the purpose, the outcomes, and the value of the role. Be specific about responsibilities, required skills, and what success looks like. If you're vague, you'll attract vague candidates. But if you're precise, you'll draw in the kind of people who know exactly what they bring to the table and how they can move your vision forward.

Do Look for Passion and Enthusiasm

It's one thing to find someone who can do the job, but it's a whole other level to find someone excited about it. Passion is the secret sauce. It's what keeps people motivated when things get tough. When you're interviewing, look for that spark— someone who's genuinely interested in your industry,

114

your mission, and the role. Passionate team members bring creativity, energy, and a 'whatever it takes' attitude that can be infectious. Trust me, enthusiasm isn't just nice to have—it's a gamechanger.

Do Prioritize Cultural Fit

You can have the most talented team in the world, but if they don't vibe together, you're in for trouble. Culture is the glue that holds a team together. Look for people who align with your core values, mission, and work style. This isn't just about liking each other; it's about shared values and mutual respect. Ask yourself: Does this person get what we're about? Will they thrive in our environment? A team that gels is a team that excels.

Do Assess Skills and Experience

Now, don't get me wrong. Passion and cultural fit are critical, but you can't forget about the skills and experience needed to get the job done. Make sure you assess whether a candidate has the chops to deliver on what you need. Do they have a proven track record? Are they adaptable? Are they willing to learn and grow within your organization? Look for both the expertise and the hunger to keep evolving.

Do Conduct Thorough Interviews

Interviewing isn't just a box to check—it's your chance to dig deep. Ask open-ended questions that go beyond the resume. Find out how they've handled real world challenges, how they approach problem-solving, and how they work with others. This is where you get to see their communication skills, their critical thinking, and whether they're a fit not just for the role but for the team. Remember, you're hiring a person, not a piece of paper.

The Don'ts of Hiring Right

Don't Rush the Hiring Process

I get it. You've got an empty seat to fill, and you want it filled yesterday. But hiring in a hurry is a rookie mistake. Take your time. Evaluate candidates thoroughly. Bring in key team members for their input. The last thing you want is to hire fast and regret faster. A rushed decision can lead to a bad hire, which costs more time, money, and energy in the long run.

Don't Neglect Reference Checks

This step isn't just a formality, it's where you find out who a candidate is when no one's watching. Skipping reference checks is like buying a car without looking under the hood. Reach out to former employers, colleagues, or anyone who can speak to the candidate's work ethic, reliability, and character. It's not about being suspicious; it's about being smart.

Don't Overlook Soft Skills

Sure, technical skills matter, but don't sleep on the soft skills—communication, teamwork, adaptability, and problem-solving. These are the qualities that will determine whether someone can navigate the real-world challenges of a growing business. You need people who can not only perform but who can also collaborate, innovate, and thrive in a dynamic environment.

Don't Forget to Consider Growth Potential

You're not just hiring for today; you're building for tomorrow. Look for candidates who have the potential to grow with your business. Are they eager to learn, ready to tackle new challenges, and capable of taking on more responsibility? A team that grows together stays together and builds something special along the way.

Don't Make Decisions Based Solely on First Impressions

First impressions can be powerful, but they're not the whole story. You need to look beyond that initial meeting and dig deeper. Don't let a charming personality or a polished resume fool you. Take the time to evaluate the full picture, the skills, the fit, the growth potential, and most importantly, the character.

Final Thought:

Building a solid team isn't just about finding people who can do the work; it's about finding the right people who align with your vision, values, and future. The do's and don'ts of hiring are not just a checklist they are the blueprint for creating a team that is capable, committed, and cohesive. A team that shares your passion, lives your values and is ready to roll up their sleeves and get to work. Don't just hire employees—build your dream team. That's how you go from good to unstoppable.

"Your business thrives when your faith is bigger than your fears."

Employee Evaluation Assessment for a Coaching Business

This assessment is designed to help you evaluate potential employees for your coaching business based on key attributes that are crucial for success in this industry. Use the table below to categorize each attribute as "Can Do Without," "Deal Breaker," or "I'd Like to Have." The last row, "How Do I Overcome," is for you to think through strategies to address any gaps or weaknesses identified in the evaluation process.

Evaluation Table

Attribute	Can Do Without	Deal Breaker	I'd Like to Have
No. 1. Strong Communication Skills			
No. 2. Understanding of Coaching Industry			
No. 3. Adaptability and Flexibility			
No. 4. Problem- Solving Ability			
No. 5. Client-Centric Mindset			
No. 6. Ability to Work Independently			
No. 7. Team Collaboration Skills			
No. 8. Sales and Marketing Experience			
No. 9. Growth-Oriented Mindset			
No. 10. Technological Proficiency			

Attribute Descriptions:

Strong Communication Skills: Ability to convey ideas clearly and effectively, both verbally and in writing.

Understanding of the Coaching Industry: Knowledge of the coaching industry, its trends, and best practices.

Adaptability and Flexibility: Capacity to adjust to changes in a fast-paced environment and handle unexpected challenges.

Problem-Solving Ability: Skill in identifying problems, analyzing options, and implementing effective solutions.

Client-Centric Mindset: Focus on understanding and meeting client needs, creating positive client experience.

Ability to Work Independently: Confidence and competence to work autonomously without needing constant supervision.

Team Collaboration Skills: Capability to work well within a team, communicate openly, and support team goals.

Sales and Marketing Experience: Experience in selling services, creating marketing strategies, and driving business growth.

Growth-Oriented Mindset: Willingness to learn, improve and take on new challenges to contribute to business success.

Technological Proficiency: Comfort and skill with using digital tools, platforms, and software relevant to the coaching business.

Roles Needed to Successfully Run a Coaching Agency

Running a successful coaching agency requires a team of skilled professionals who can manage various aspects of the business, from client acquisition to program delivery and operational management. Below is a comprehensive list of essential roles, each with a job title, job description, and typical pay ranges.

1. Head Coach / Lead Coach

Job Description: The Head Coach is responsible for designing coaching programs, delivering high-quality coaching sessions, and overseeing the performance of other coaches. They act as the face of the agency and ensure that all coaching services align with the agency's mission and values.

Key Responsibilities:

Develop and deliver coaching programs and workshops.

Oversee and mentor other coaches within the agency.

Maintain relationships with high-value clients.

Evaluate client progress and adjust coaching strategies as needed.

Pay Range: $80,000 - $150,000 per year, depending on experience and location.

2. Client Success Manager

Job Description: The Client Success Manager ensures that clients have seamless experience with the coaching agency. They manage client onboarding, monitor client satisfaction, and act as liaisons between clients and coaches.

Key Responsibilities:

Onboard new clients and ensure they understand the coaching process.

Regularly check in with clients to monitor satisfaction and progress.

Coordinate between clients and coaches to ensure goals are met.

Manage client retention strategies and address any issues promptly.

Pay Range: $50,000 - $80,000 per year.

3. Marketing and Content Manager

Job Description: The Marketing and Content Manager develops and implements marketing strategies to attract new clients and promote the coaching agency's brand. They are responsible for content creation, social media management, email marketing, and lead generation.

Key Responsibilities:

Create and manage content for blogs, social media, email campaigns, and the agency's website.

Develop and execute marketing strategies to attract and retain clients.

Manage SEO, PPC, and social media advertising campaigns.

Track and analyze marketing performance metrics.

Pay Range: $55,000 - $90,000 per year.

4. Sales Consultant / Enrollment Specialist

Job Description: The Sales Consultant is responsible for converting leads into clients. They conduct consultations with potential clients to understand their needs, present coaching programs, and close sales.

Key Responsibilities:

Conduct sales consultations and follow-up with potential clients.

Understand client needs and present tailored coaching solutions.

Achieve monthly and quarterly sales targets.

Maintain and update the CRM with clients and lead information.

Pay Range: $45,000 - $85,000 per year (base salary + commission).

5. Operations Manager

Job Description: The Operations Manager oversees the daily operations of the coaching agency, ensuring efficiency and productivity. They manage resources, coordinate with different departments, and ensure that processes are streamlined.

Key Responsibilities:

Oversee day-to-day operations, including scheduling, client management, and staff coordination.

Develop and implement standard operating procedures.

Ensure compliance with legal and regulatory requirements.

Manage budgets, resources, and financial performance.

Pay Range: $65,000 - $110,000 per year.

6. Content Creator / Copywriter

Job Description: The Content Creator develops engaging content to support marketing and client engagement efforts. This includes blog posts, eBooks, social media updates, email sequences, and more.

Key Responsibilities:

Write and edit compelling content for digital and print media

Collaborate with the marketing team to develop content strategies.

Create content that drives engagement and promotes brand awareness.

Ensure all content aligns with the agency's voice and values.

Pay Range: $40,000 - $70,000 per year.

7. Social Media Manager

Job Description: The Social Media Manager is responsible for managing all social media platforms and engaging with the audience. They create content, schedule posts, analyze engagement, and run paid social media campaigns.

Key Responsibilities:

Develop and implement social media strategies across multiple platforms.

Engage with followers, respond to comments, and manage the community.

Create, schedule, and analyze social media content.

Run social media ad campaigns and optimize for performance.

Pay Range: $45,000 - $75,000 per year.

8. Administrative Assistant

Job Description: The Administrative Assistant provides administrative support to the coaching agency's leadership and coaches. They manage scheduling, handle client communications, and assist with day-to-day tasks.

Key Responsibilities:

Manage schedules, book appointments, and handle cancellations.

Respond to client inquiries and support onboarding processes.

Maintain records, files, and databases.

Assist in organizing events, workshops, and meetings.

Pay Range: $35,000 - $55,000 per year.

9. Technical Support Specialist

Job Description: The Technical Support Specialist ensures that all technology-related aspects of the coaching agency run smoothly. They manage the agency's website, handle technical issues, and support the implementation of digital tools and platforms.

Key Responsibilities:

Maintain and update the agency's website and digital platforms.

Troubleshoot technical issues for staff and clients.

Assist in implementing new technologies and software tools.

Ensure data security and compliance with digital regulations.

Pay Range: $50,000 - $80,000 per year.

10. Program Coordinator

Job Description: The Program Coordinator manages the logistics of coaching programs, workshops, and events. They ensure all programs run smoothly and that clients receive the resources and support they need.

Key Responsibilities:

Coordinate and manage the scheduling of coaching sessions and events.

Communicate with clients to provide program updates and resources.

Collaborate with coaches to ensure program delivery meets agency standards.

Handle logistics for in-person and virtual events.

Pay Range: $45,000 - $70,000 per year.

Final Thoughts:

These roles, when filled by the right people, will form the backbone of a successful coaching agency. They cover all essential aspects—coaching delivery, client success, marketing, sales, operations, content creation, and technical support— ensuring that the agency runs smoothly, effectively, and profitably. The pay ranges provided are based on industry standards and may vary depending on location, experience, and agency size.

"A premium brand isn't built overnight; it's crafted daily with intention and consistency."

Chapter 8: Mastering High Ticket Sales for Coaches

Let's get one thing straight: when it comes to selling high-ticket coaching programs, you don't "sell." You offer people an opportunity – a chance to transform their lives, their businesses, and their futures. But it has to be an opportunity that aligns with their deepest needs, one that they're ready and willing to invest in. When you approach sales with integrity, confidence, and a method that feels genuine, you don't have to be a "salesperson." You just have to be a guide.

I've seen many coaches struggle with sales because they think it's about convincing, pushing, or manipulating people into buying. Let me tell you right now— if that's your mindset, you're in the wrong game. I've built a multiple seven figure coaching business not by selling, but by providing value and presenting solutions. I never sell someone something I haven't done myself. And that's the key to high-ticket sales: authentic, value-driven conversations.

We're going to dive deep into a powerful sales process that I've used to consistently close high-ticket coaching clients. This process is not just about making the sale; it's about connecting, understanding, and providing a solution that feels like a no-brainer. Let's break it down step-by-step.

Step 1: Set the Tone and Take Control at the Start of the Call

The first thing you need to understand is that **taking control of the call from the very beginning is one of the most critical steps in high-ticket sales.** Why? Because this sets the tone for the entire conversation. When you open the call confidently, you establish yourself as the authority, the expert, and the guide.

You're not there to be their friend; you're there to solve their problem.

How do you take control? Start by outlining the structure of the call. Let the prospect know that you're going to ask some questions to understand their situation better, then, if it makes sense, you'll talk about what working together could look like. By setting this agenda, you're letting them know that this isn't a casual chat. It's a serious, professional conversation with a clear purpose.

When you take control, you avoid falling into the trap of letting the prospect lead the call with their questions or objections. You're not there to react; you're there to direct. When prospects feel that confidence from you, they're more likely to open up and share their real challenges, which gives you the insight you need to position your offer later on.

Step 2: Build Rapport and Create a Safe Space

Now, just because you're in control doesn't mean you're not building rapport. In fact, rapport is essential. But we're not talking about fake rapport—the "How's the weather?" kind of small talk that doesn't go anywhere. Real rapport is about creating a safe space where the prospect feels comfortable opening up.

Ask questions that matter. Questions that dive deep into what's going on in their life or business. You want them to feel seen, heard and understood. When you can articulate their problem better than they can, you position yourself as the obvious solution. Remember, the key to rapport isn't just about being liked; it's about trust.

And trust is built by showing them you understand their world and their challenges.

When you create this safe space, they'll let their guard down, and that's where the magic happens. That's when they'll tell you their real fears, their real desires, and their real obstacles. And that's the goldmine of information you'll need to show them why your coaching is the answer.

Step 3: Dig Deep and Diagnose the Real Problem

Once you've got rapport, it's time to dig deep. Too many coaches make the mistake of staying on the surface—talking about superficial problems without getting to the root cause. But you're not here to solve surface-level issues. You're here to provide deep, transformative solutions.

Start asking questions that get to the core. What's holding them back? Why haven't they been able to solve this on their own? What's the impact on their life if they don't fix this now? This is where you go from being a coach to being a detective. You're piecing together their story to identify the real problem—the problem that, when solved, will create a profound impact.

And here's the thing: most people don't even know what their real problem is.

They think they do, but they don't. That's why they need you. Your job is to connect the dots for them, to show them the gap between where they are and where they want to be. And then you become the bridge that gets them there.

Step 4: Amplify the Pain and the Cost of Inaction

Listen, people don't move unless they feel a compelling reason to. And sometimes, that reason is pain. No, we're not talking about manipulation. We're talking about helping them see the true cost of staying stuck. What does it cost them emotionally, financially, physically, and relationally to not take action?

You've got to get them to see that the pain of staying the same is greater than the pain of change. Help them understand the stakes—what happens if nothing changes? What does another year of inaction look like for them? Sometimes it's not about introducing something new, but rather helping them realize what they've already been losing.

By amplifying the pain, you help them realize that the time to act is now. You're not pushing them; you're waking them up. And sometimes, that's exactly what they need.

Step 5: Position Your Offer as the Solution

Once you've diagnosed the real problem and amplified the pain, it's time to position your offer as the solution. But here's the twist—you're not selling. You're simply presenting a professional recommendation. You've done the work to understand their needs, and now you're providing a solution that meets those needs.

Think of it like this: You're the doctor, and they're the patient. You don't "sell" them on a treatment; you prescribe it. You explain exactly what your coaching program can do for them, how it works, and why it's the right fit based on everything they've told you.

Keep it simple. Don't overcomplicate it. They're not buying features—they're buying results. Speak directly to their pain points and how your coaching is the bridge to their desired outcome. If you've done your job right up to this point, this should feel like the most natural step in the world.

Step 6: Handle Objections with Confidence and Empathy

Objections are part of the process. They're not a sign that the prospect isn't interested; they're a sign that they're considering. When objections come up, you don't get defensive, and you certainly don't back down. You handle them with confidence and empathy.

Listen to their concerns. Validate their feelings. Then, reframe those objections in a way that brings them back to the value of the solution you're offering. For example, if they say, "I'm not sure I have the time," you might respond, "I understand. That's exactly why this coaching program is structured to help you create more time and efficiency in your business."

It's not about fighting the objection; it's about understanding the root of it and addressing it in a way that feels supportive, not combative. And remember, objections are a good sign. They show that the prospect is engaged in the conversation and is weighing the decision seriously.

Step 7: Close by Offering an Opportunity, Not a Sale

Now comes the close. But here's the thing—**we don't close to sell; we close to give people an opportunity to buy.** You're not selling; you're inviting them to take the next step in their journey. You're offering them the chance to invest in themselves, to make a decision that aligns with their highest good.

Always remember, you never sell someone something that you haven't done yourself, and you always sell with integrity. If your coaching program doesn't fulfill their need, don't offer it. The right clients will see the value, feel the alignment, and make the decision that's best for them.

And when you close, do it with confidence. Use assumptive language—"Here's what happens next…" or "Let's get you started…" Make it clear that you believe in the solution you're providing and that you're ready to guide them every step of the way.

Step 8: Confirm the Commitment and Set Expectations

Once the prospect agrees, it's time to confirm their commitment and set clear expectations. Let them know what the next steps are, what they can expect from you, and what you expect from them. This isn't just about closing a sale; it's about beginning a partnership.

When you set expectations early, you create a foundation of trust and accountability. This is where you lay out the framework for the transformation they're about to embark on. Make sure they're fully aware of the commitment they're making, both in terms of time and effort.

Final Thoughts: Selling with Integrity and Confidence

High-ticket sales aren't about tricks or gimmicks; they're about genuine, value driven conversations that empower people to make decisions that change their lives. When you approach sales from a place of integrity, when you focus on solving real problems and providing real value, the sales process becomes seamless.

Remember, you're not just closing deals; you're opening doors. Doors to transformation, growth, and limitless potential. You're not just making money; you're making a difference. And when you sell with that mindset, you'll see how effortless and rewarding high-ticket sales can truly be.

Go out there, have those conversations, and give people the opportunity to say yes to the life they've been dreaming of. Because that's what we do—we change lives, one decision at a time.

"If you don't see yourself as a leader, neither will your clients."

Your Journey to Mastery Has Just Begun

All right, my friend, you've made it to the end of this book. But let me tell you something, this isn't the end; it's just the beginning. You've journeyed through these chapters, and I hope you've felt every word. I hope you've seen yourself in these pages, faced your challenges head-on, and started thinking about your coaching business in a whole new way.

We started this journey by looking at how to **"Reflect, Refocus, Rebuild"**— where you learned how to dig deep and understand where you're missing the mark, not as a way to beat yourself up, but as a way to build up and come back stronger than ever. You've got to know where you've been to know where you're going, and that starts with honest self-assessment.

Then, we dove into the art of becoming truly relentless. **"Forge an Unbreakable Mindset"** taught you how to tap into the power God put inside you. You see, God didn't create another you, and He didn't make any mistakes when He made you. When you lean into who He created you to be, there's nothing that can stop you. Failure is just fuel, and we don't quit when things get tough—we double down.

We explored **"Know Your Audience"** because if you're trying to speak to everybody, you're speaking to nobody. You've got to know who you're called to serve. Just like a marksman at the range, you aim for the bullseye, but you'll still hit other spots on the target. That's how your message lands with power—by knowing exactly who you're speaking to and what they need to hear from you.

I showed you how to **"Develop Your Story"** because your story is the foundation of your brand. Your story isn't just a part of your business; it IS your business. It's what connects you to your clients on a deep, human level. It's what turns a 'maybe' into a 'yes.' Remember, people don't buy coaching; they buy transformation. And that transformation starts with your story.

Then, we got into **"Building Your Premium Coaching Brand."** It's not just about fancy logos or catchy taglines—it's about creating an experience. Your brand is what people say about you when you're

141

not in the room. It's the promise you make and keep. We looked at giants like Apple, Gucci, and Jay-Z and broke down why their brands demand attention and dollars. And we asked the tough questions about what makes your brand stand out in a crowded market.

We didn't stop there. We laid out the **"Cash Flow Revenue Generation Strategy,"** where we broke down the entire Value Ladder. From your entry-level offers to your premium one-on-one coaching, we went deep into how to create offers that feel irresistible. We talked about moving clients up the ladder step-by-step, adding value at every level, and building a solid, recurring revenue model that keeps your cash flow steady and strong. I shared how I've done this in my own business and how I teach my clients to do the same.

And we closed out with the real deal on **"High-Ticket Sales."** We went deep into how to take control of the conversation from the very start, build genuine rapport, dig deep to diagnose the real problem, and position your offer as the solution. I reminded you that we don't sell— we give people the opportunity to buy. We sell with integrity. We guide people toward the transformation they need, and we only offer them what we know will deliver.

Now, here's where the rubber meets the road. Reading this book is one thing but putting it into action is another. You've got the blueprint, but now it's time to build. I don't just want you to take what you've learned and let it collect dust on the shelf. I want you to move. I want you to act. I want you to go out there and CRUSH IT.

That's why I'm inviting you to take the next step with me. If you're serious about leveling up your coaching business and standing out and crushing sales in a crowded market, join www.joindrsuber.com in **The Cash Flow Blueprint for Coaches Webinar**. This isn't just another webinar; it's a transformation. We're going to take these concepts, dive even deeper, and put them into action. I'm going to walk you through every step of building a business that not only stands out but dominates.

Or, if you're ready to go even deeper, work with me directly. I've helped countless coaches scale to multiple six and seven figures, and I'd love to help you do the same. But let's be clear—I only work with coaches who are ready to do the work, committed, and relentless about their success.

So, what's it going to be? Are you going to sit on this krowledge and let it slip away, or are you going to take the next step and change the game? The choice is yours, but know this—if you're ready, I'm here for you and ready to go all in with you. Let's build something extraordinary together.

Stay relentless,
Dr. Jamar Suber

Your Coach and Partner in Success

"Clarity in your vision attract clarity in your clientele."

Meet Dr. Jamar Suber

Dr. Jamar Suber: Empowering Coaches and Entrepreneurs to Unleash Their Full Potential

Dr. Jamar Suber is a dynamic business strategist, brand development expert, and high-ticket sales coach with a powerful story of resilience and transformation. Rising from the gritty streets of Pittsburgh, Dr. Suber has built a multiple seven figure coaching empire by combining decades of business tactics with deep spiritual wisdom. He specializes in helping high-net-worth coaches and consultants scale their businesses, build premium brands, and generate consistent cash flow with integrity.

As a sought-after speaker, Dr. Suber captivates audiences with his authentic, no-nonsense approach to success. He is the creator of "The Cash Flow Blueprint for Coaches," a proven system that empowers entrepreneurs to stand out in crowded markets and crush sales. With his Four Pillars to Success—Faith, Family, Finances, and Fortitude—at the core of his message, Dr. Suber inspires and equips others to lead lives of purpose, impact, and relentless pursuit of their goals.

Book Dr. Jamar Suber for your next event and give your audience the tools they need to transform their mindset, their business, and their future.

Have Questions? Book A Call with Dr. Suber For Your VIP Business Audit Today - VIP Business Audit Call

"Your first client is always you—believe in what you offer, and the world will follow."

Partners

Plush Hair and Skin - https://plushhairandskin.co/

Vibes Ink Jax - https://vibes-ink.com/

Influence & Authority Digital Media Strategy https://iadigitalstrategy.com/

#iamtheboss - https://iamboss.shop/

Have Questions? Book A Call with Dr. Suber for Your VIP Business Audit Today! VIP Business Audit Call

www.ingramcontent.com/pod-product-compliance
Lightning Source LLC
Chambersburg PA
CBHW060536130626
46553CB00002B/775